EARN THAT SEAT
PRACTICAL HELP FROM THE GUY
TO WIN AN ELECTION

Featuring 107 American Flag Photos
And The Voices of Dedicated Public Servants

Copyright © 2017

By Michael Gold

All Rights Reserved.
ISBN-13- 978-1540765727
ISBN-10- 1540765725 Library of Congress Control Number: 2016920199
CreateSpace Independent Publishing Platform, North Charleston, SC

Dedicated to my greatest loves:

Linnie, my incredible, beautiful, supportive wife; Gabrielle and Arianne, my extraordinary, loving daughters who don't think I'm the best dressed guy in the world; Juniper and Magnolia, the smartest, most beautiful granddaughters in the world (what else?); Ethan, my terrific, athletic, smart, sweet grandson; and Dane and Charlie, the best sons-in-law one could be lucky enough to simply call sons.

They got my vote!

PREFACE

It all started here:

When I was a small boy growing up in the tiny village of Woodridge, NY, of perhaps seven or eight hundred people, I remember my grandparents' front porch on Maple Avenue and the magnet it was for all of their neighboring friends.

My Grandparents' house on Maple Avenue, Woodridge, NY, now deserted

In the spring and summer, night after night, people gathered and sat in the warm darkness; there were no street lights then, their cigarette and cigar smoke softly swirling and filling the air with its pungency to accompany the laughter and sarcasm and political banter from all those shadowed voices.

Life in a microcosm of America, of first and second generation immigrants whose lifeblood, besides all the family stories all had to share, was politics, politics, politics. People leaned forward on their chairs, gesturing vigorously and stridently to make their points, both about local politicians and national.

My grandfather, the village blacksmith, always with his wide-brimmed cap on, and his pinochle cohorts, were relentless in their arguments and humorous in their good-natured put-downs. I most often sat next to my grandfather, not really understanding all the words from their foreign language, but reveling in their camaraderie and infectious laughter. My grandfather was my hero. I watched him still shoeing horses in his later years. I pumped his forge and hammered on his anvil and wondered who Michael J. Quill was, that stern-faced, bald guy whose poster hung in Pop's blacksmith shop.

Later on, I learned what a tough sonofabitch labor organizer for the TWU Mr. Quill was. No wonder my grandfather liked him.

When I reached 9th grade, I was elected President of my class and in 12th I became the Athletic Association President. My best friend was 12th grade Class President and I helped get him elected. My grandfather was very proud of me. It meant everything.

Throughout my career, I have photographed a never-ending number of political incumbents and candidates, endless political events, strategized on local campaigns and was part of a think tank for platform decisions for a town supervisor's race.

I've photographed a Vice-President of the United States, Governors, US Senators, Congressmen, Judges, District Attorneys, County Executives, Mayors, Councilmen/women, and so on.

One of my very first assignments for The New York Times Magazine was a cover photo of the late Carter Burden and his then wife, Amanda Paley Burden. In other words, I've had the opportunity of observing and speaking with an endless stream of public servants.

"Earn That Vote" is a very different, unconventional book on helping candidates get elected. It's not a textbook. It relies mostly on the political experiences and wisdom of dedicated public servants whom I've interviewed. They relate how their families, life experiences and obstacles they've had to overcome influenced them to get into politics and devoted public service.

Read the *"Voices"* section carefully, and you will begin to understand why political people altruistically have a deep desire to help others in need. *"Earn That Vote"* also includes my own thoughts and insight into the world of politics.

It is raw, direct, unblinking, tough, honest, realistic, practical, smart,
and is the most important book you'll ever read on grassroots politics to help you get elected.
I hope it will help get YOU to the finish line — FIRST!

AGENDA

DEDICATION AND PREFACE - 5-8

INTRODUCTION — Pg.10- 26 The Beauty and Gift of American Grassroots Democracy, as Well as Voices from Dedicated Public Servants

Chapter 1 — Pg. 27-29 The Eternal Quest for Victory — **Winning is Everything ✪ Inner Conviction ✪ Inner Drive**

CHAPTER 2 — Pg. 30-36 Ego, Power and Passion — The Political Personality ✪ Love of Combat ✪ Why Are You Running? ✪ What Drives You? ✪ Heroic or Billy Goat? ✪ Look In the Mirror

CHAPTER 3 — Pg. 37-43 THE "COME TO JESUS MOMENT" — Skeletons ✪ "Building a Bench" ✪ Questions For Campaign managers and Strategists ✪ Giver or Taker? ✪ Support

CHAPTER 4 — Pg. 44-55 THE CAMPAIGN MANAGER: A MAESTRO TO CONDUCT THE ORCHESTRA — Believing In Your Candidate ✪ Campaign Strategist ✪ Fixing Potholes ✪ "Mother'$ Milk" ✪ Campaign Narrative ✪ "The Green Team"

CHAPTER 5 — Pg.56-59 **DO YOU REALLY NEED A CONSULTANT?** — Interviewing a Consultant ✪ Consultants are Not Gods ✪ Coke/Pepsi- It's All a Game

CHAPTER 6 — Pg. 60-68 **THE ABSOLUTE IMPORTANCE OF YOUR BOARD OF ELECTIONS** — Plan a Visit ✪ Make Nice ✪ Rules ✪ Deadlines ✪ Contributions✪Petitions ✪ Absentee Ballots ✪ "It's No Fun to Lose, So Don't Lose"

CHAPTER 7 — Pg. 69-73 **IT'S WHO YA KNOW** ✪ Creating an organization ✪ Endorsements and Testimonials ✪ Building Relationships ✪Don't Sell Your Soul ✪ Go To Church, Synagogue or Mosque ✪Priorities & Petitions ✪ Reading newspapers ✪ Lists of Perceived Campaign Issues

CHAPTER 8 — Pg. 74-81 **FINANCE COMMITTEE- MONEY MAKES THE WORLD GO 'ROUND, BUT NOT ALWAYS** — "Access Capital" ✪ Campaign Contribution Limits ✪ Housekeeping Money ✪ Keeping Kosher ✪ Strict Accounting and Reporting

CHAPTER 9 — Pg. 82-84 **CREATING AN ORGANIZATION** — Building a Staff ✪ Researching The Important Issues ✪ Platform ✪ Be Arrogant — Don't Listen ✪ The Key to The Kingdom

CHAPTER 10 — Pg. 85-89 **THE CANDIDATE MUST SHOW UP** — The Need For a Scheduler ✪ Speaking at Fails and Festivals ✪ Walk the Parades ✪ AWOL ✪ Do Your Homework ✪ Include and Compliment

CHAPTER 11 — Pg. 90-92 **OH, WHAT A BEAUTIFUL BABY!** — The Birth of Your Platform and Kitchen Cabinet ✪ Visiting Individual Communities ✪ Listening, Two Ways of Talking to People

CHAPTER 12 — Pg. 93-101 **JUDICIAL CAMPAIGNS MUST TAKE THE HIGH ROAD** — Remembering a master Listener-in-Chief ✪ Forbidden to Speak Negatively of Your Opponent ✪ Blind Contributions ✪ Window Period ✪ Campaign Literature and Handouts ✪ Sample Letter to Constituents

CHAPTER 13— Pg. 102-107 **VOLUNTEERS: YES, I CAN, YES, I CAN, YES, I CAN!** — Recruiting Volunteers, ✪ Volunteer Skills ✪ Boots on the Ground ✪ Scripts ✪ Volunteer Coordinator ✪ Showing Your Appreciation ✪ Hugs ✪ Food ✪ Certificates and Photos Go a Long Way

CHAPTER 14 — Pg. 108-111 REACHING OUT & SWEATING THE SMALL STUFF — Long-Range Strategy ✪ Key Players ✪ Reaching Out ✪ Chumming the Water ✪ Meeting Local Officials ✪ Business Organizations ✪ Political Party groups ✪ Social Groups and Organizations ✪ Building a personal Data Base ✪ Polling

CHAPTER 15 — Pg. 112-114 THE APHRODISIAC OF POWER — Owning the Room ✪ Sink or Swim ✪ Be a Schmoozer ✪ Bring Cute Kids ✪ Body Language and Looking Them In the Eye ✪ Humility

CHAPTER 16 — Pg. 115-116 SECRET WEAPON #1 — Spouses or Significant Others ✪ Sainthood ✪ Loneliness ✪ Companionship ✪ Eating Home ✪ Drinking a Glass of Wine ✪ Reading Bedtime Stories

CHAPTER 17 — Pg. 117-119 SECRET WEAPON #2: SNOWBIRDS, COLLEGES & THE MILITARY. THEY VOTE, TOO, YOU KNOW — Importance of Absentee Ballots, Board of Elections Sample Mail-In Ballot, Targets, The Difference They Make

CHAPTER 18 — Pg. 120-123 THE ABSOLUTE POWER OF A PROPER HANDSHAKE, KISSES & THE BIG SQUEEZE — Hit The Bricks ✪ Pressing the Flesh ✪ Asking Store Owners For their Permission ✪ Crushers ✪ Courtesy ✪ MWAH ✪ Selfies ✪ Peanut Butter and Jelly First

CHAPTER 19 — Pg. 124 EAT FISH/DON'T EAT FISH: THE GREAT DEBATE — Yes! No! Never!

CHAPTER 20 — Pg. 125-126 POLITICAL PHEROMONES — Being Loved ✪ Sharing the Wealth ✪ Compliments and Meet and Greet

CHAPTER 21 — Pg. 127-128 WHERE'S THE CANDIDATE? CAN'T SEE OR HEAR HIM OR HER. WHAT DID HE SAY? — Preparing to Speak ✪ Lights and Microphone ✪ Surveying the Room ✪ Love Your Audience ✪ Sincerity ✪ Researching the Important Issues

CHAPTER 22 — Pg. 129-131 THE BOY SCOUT MOTTO: BE PREPARED, PLUS A LOT MORE — Making Yourself Available to the Press ✪ Practicing Answers to Questions ✪ Ad Articles ✪ Three Point Shots ✪ Listen ✪ Man Up

CHAPTER 23 — Pg. 132-136 NEGATIVE CAMPAIGNING — Kill 'em In the Crib ✪ Dirty Politics ✪ Bad Apples ✪ Whisper Campaigns ✪ Power @#$%^&! ✪ Being Aware ✪ Smartphones ✪ Videos and Hidden Mics

CHAPTER 24 — Pg. 137-145 **WHO'S THAT KNOCKIN' AT MY DOOR?** — Bloody Knuckles ✪ In the Middle of a Dog ✪ Dressing Properly ✪ Name Tags ✪ Hide That Watch/Car ✪ Body Language ✪ Giveaways ✪ Bingo

CHAPTER 25 — Pg. 146-151 **THE WHOLE MESSAGE AND NOTHING BUT THE WHOLE MESSAGE AND "DEAR NAME" LETTERS** — Fliers ✪ Palm Cards ✪ Content ✪ Personal Letters ✪ Logos ✪ Relationship with Printers ✪ Tight Deadlines ✪ Chef Mikey's WINNING Campaign Bread Recipe ✪ Sample Letter to Friends and Strangers ✪ A Little Sugar

CHAPTER 26 — Pg. 152-153 **THAT OMG BEAUTIFUL SMILE FOR THE CAMERA** — Headshots and Love At First Sight ✪ Backdrops ✪ Lighting ✪ Bald Heads ✪ Hairdo ✪ Glasses

CHAPTER 27 — Pg. 154-155 **POWER POSES & MICHAELANGELO'S STATUE OF DAVID (At Least the Face)** — Contrapposto ✪ Power Poses ✪ Smile or Not? ✪ Ask Yog ✪ Digital Plastic Surgery ✪ A Retouching Refrain ✪ Reminder to Photographers- Privacy Importance

CHAPTER 28 — Pg. 156-159 **POWER CLOTHES & CAMPAIGN APPEARANCE** — Clothing Styles and Colors ✪ Don't Underdress ✪ Don't Overdo Makeup ✪ No Sex ✪ On-Location setting and Outfits ✪ Receiving Awards

CHAPTER 29 — Pg. 160-167 **THE POWER OF THE WEB & DO-IT-YOURSELF VIDEOS** — Importance of Your Website ✪ Facebook ✪ YouTube ✪ Twitte ✪ Snapchat ✪ Pinterest ✪ Linkedin ✪ Announcing Your Candidacy ✪ Getting Your Message and Platform Out ✪ Lots of Technical Information ✪ Counteracting Social Media Lies

CHAPTER 30 — Pg. 168 **THE SHORTEST & MOST IMPORTANT CHAPTER YOU WILL EVER READ** — The Magic Words

CHAPTER 31 — Pg. 169-171 **THE DAY OF RECKONING, ELECTION DAY** — The Difference Between Winning and Losing ✪ Getting Out the Vote ✪ Handing Out Literature At the Polling Stations ✪ Dressing Appropriately ✪ Putting On a Smile

CHAPTER 32 — Pg. 172-174 **LEAVE NO VOTE UNTURNED** — Being Present When the Votes Are Counted ✪ Count Those Absentee Ballots ✪ Manning the Phones With Reminders ✪ Providing Transportation ✪ Last Minute Speeches

CHAPTER 33 — Pg. 175 **A TOAST TO THE WINNERS** — Steve Jobs ✪ The Legacy you Will Leave

LIST OF CONTRIBUTORS- Pg. 176

The Beauty And Gift Of Grassroots American Democracy At Your Service:

See Dick Run.
Run, Dick, Run.
Run, Run, Run.
See Jane Run.
Run, Jane, Run.
Run, Run, Run.
- Excerpt by William S. Gray and Zerna Sharp

Win, Dick, Win.
Win, Jane, Win.
Win, Win, Win.

VOICES

In America, we've grown up bestowing honor upon our country's historical heroes; Washington, Jefferson, Lincoln, Roosevelt, MLK, Jr. and so many more. They have framed our sense of patriotism and pride in America and in the beauty and gift of democracy we so cherish.

But our greatest heroes and most influential "parents" are those who are the closest people to us. They're not the abstract heroes we've learned to love, but rather, our real parents, grandparents, siblings, aunts and uncles, teachers, mentors, first employers, who've taught us about life, have gone to war to protect us, and who've prepared us for our future.

They've made us toe the line, accept responsibility, be accountable, taught us the importance of integrity and kindness, service, true patriotism, contribution to society and above all, love of family and neighbors in our communities. In other words, they've not only looked out for themselves and their own families, they've looked out for others, selflessly. Those are the people we've looked to and continue to celebrate as we go through life.

Theirs are the voices, filled with grassroots wisdom, that we continue to hear over our shoulders, and they are always in our hearts. This book is a celebration of them and does honor to our system of government, as complicated and as frustrating as it can be. But in the end, in America, they represent the best of who we are and what we hold so dear.

Here are a few of those voices that have already made a difference and continue to do so, and I am honored that they've given of themselves for the betterment of this book.

Michael Gold

VOICES OF DEDICATED PUBLIC SERVANTS

Michael P. Hein: "There are some moments in leadership that are very special. Moments where you are able to make significant and meaningful change that profoundly benefits the people you represent. And it is these moments that transcend partisan politics and make all the challenges worthwhile. As a reformer that's what I believe public service is all about.

"And to create more successful accomplishments, you have to be a person of conviction and put to use your capacity to effectuate real change and do everything you can to build partnerships in the process in order to make it a reality. And so sometimes, the bricks fall over and you have to pick them up and build again and if you do it long enough, brick by brick, you will have then built something that's extraordinary."
-Michael P. Hein, county executive, Ulster County, NY

Christopher Gibson: "I'm an idealist. I believe in our country. I think that's why we're here. People ask 'Why are we here?' What is this to me? I think why we're here is that we actually help to complete God because, can you imagine perfection without imperfection? It can't be done. Right? And you know, we have free will and when we use our free will to help others, we're rewarded. That one feeling you get when you help somebody, we call 'euphoria.' You just know it. When you get that, euphoria is actually a connection to God. And so, when we make a difference for our fellow man, when we serve others, when we actually help the body politic to reach a higher level, we are not only personally rewarded, but we actually help make this connection between the perfect and the imperfect because we have free will to get there, and we thus serve God.

"My service provides a voice for people, regardless of party, regardless of how they vote, and I hope they vote, but even if they don't, I'm their voice that can ultimately not only change public policy for the better, but restore our faith in our ability to be self-governing; a government of the people, by the people, for the people."
-Christopher Gibson, congressman, U.S. House of Representatives, 19th District, NY

Anthony T. Kane: "What motivated me to run for judicial office was the unsuitability of the candidates who were being proposed for that particular court. "The judicial system in this country has no police force, has no army, it can't pass laws, it can't raise money, it is dependent for its existence on the other two branches of government. Its strength derives from the reasonableness and sense of justice of the court's decisions and its power resides in the public perception that the courts are doing justice. If the public loses trust in the courts it is possible for the legislative or executive branch to disregard the court system and diminish its powers.

Courthouse, New York City

"I always knew for whom I worked. I worked for the people who relied upon the court system. They were the people who hired me (by election), paid me (by their tax revenue), who trusted me, who put their lives into my hands. If the orders a court issues are going to have any impact they must not only appear to be just they must be just within the rule of law. Judges must listen to the arguments of the parties and support their determinations in well reasoned written decisions. When I followed this process I found that the litigants usually accepted the decision even if they disagreed and were unhappy with the result." -Anthony T. Kane, judge of the Supreme Court of the State of New York and formerly family court judge, Sullivan County, NY. (retired)

Elliott Auerbach: "I think the nature of who I am came from my family's influence. I learned a real valuable lesson along the way: That you look at someone and everyone is truly the same. Whether they come from wealth, or they come from poverty, whether they worked hard all their lives, or they were born with a golden spoon, you treat everybody the same, and it really is a common denominator on how you personally behave and how you behave with other people.

"It boils down to, really, a simple phrase, 'Whose life can I change today?' I wake up in the morning and ask, whom can I help and how can I make a difference? Who's that one individual or that one group of individuals whose life or lives I can change just by being there as a public servant, whether I am a solution to their problems or the conduit that helps them toward the solution of whatever problem they may have.

"So if you've helped somebody out like that, you can't quantify that. It's a sense of fulfillment inside you. I always say I'm a runner. I'm not the fastest runner and I'll never win the New York Marathon, and the older I become, the longer the mile has gotten, so that with age, it's that personal inner feeling when you have that personal best, that personal accomplishment. And that is what winning the Peoples' Marathon really is. It's running that extra mile."
-Elliott Auerbach, comptroller, Ulster County, NY

Adele B. Reiter: "I have a deep respect for public office and the inherent responsibilities that come with it. There are qualities that I believe are essential for anyone who wants to serve their community by holding public office. In order to make a positive difference in the lives of the people who elected them and work to improve the country we all love, an individual must possess key qualities such as: perseverance, strength of conviction and courage to do the right thing, intelligence, kindness, and a passion for good government.

"For myself, I can say this; governing is difficult work, but it is important and fulfilling work. I strive to make the community better for my family, my friends, my neighbors and all those who choose to live here. That includes working to help prevent people from being taxed out of their homes, and on-going efforts to attract new businesses to the area so people can find jobs close to home. I have learned that to be effective while serving in government it is critical to clearly communicate what you will do for the public good, recognize that it is the right thing to do, and have a realistic plan to do it.

"To achieve that, you must remember why you made this choice in the first place. You must achieve your goals and live up to your ideals, while mastering the art of compromise. But most importantly, you must stand strong when it is called for in order to deliver results for the people who put their faith and trust in you."
-Adele B. Reiter, deputy county executive and chief of staff, Ulster County, NY

Richard Croce: "The thing that jumps to my mind immediately was the way my mother brought us up. She was very strict, in that we had to be respectful, and being a large family, we had to think of others before ourselves. Whatever we did had to be for the benefit of the group, meaning our family and siblings.

"There were fourteen of us and I was number two, so I had to do just about anything in the house; change diapers, do laundry, cook meals. We all had jobs and had to be home by 5 o'clock every day to perform our duties for the day up into the evening, including setting the table, clearing the table, doing the dishes. There was no dishwasher.

"During dry times, droughts, our well would run dry and then we had to take milk cans about a mile away and fill them using an outdoor hand pump. It was very difficult. We had an outhouse we had to use that was there just for these emergencies. Unisex!
There were two tables in the kitchen: My father had a table made for ten of us and my parents sat at the smaller table for themselves and the two youngest boys. It was a picnic table that was extra wide and long. It had a Formica top for easy cleaning. Everything was done in that room; our homework, everything. It was the family room. TV was done in the living room, but there wasn't that much TV back then and we watched very little of it. There wasn't much time, anyhow, to watch.
We had a commercial milk machine like you would have in a restaurant. You would lift the handles up for the milk and it was filled from the metal milk cans. Farm cans. They used to come three times a week. We had pitchers of milk on the table during meal times for everyone.

"But I didn't think that life was a hardship. There were clothes that were handed down. 'Course, I was one of the oldest, so I never got a hand-me-down.

"We grew up with a sense of responsibility. The house couldn't function if we didn't follow what we were supposed to do. There had to be a certain routine in the house that had to be followed so things would go smoothly. It wasn't just going to happen. It was set up and you did it and the older ones took care of the younger ones to help our mother out. It wasn't like babysitting, 'cause they never went out. Maybe later in life they went out without any of us kids and then to family functions, which we all attended.

"As it relates to helping other people, my father was very involved in different organizations. He was a member of the Lions Club, and he and my mother were two of the people who originated the rescue squad in Modena (NY). I don't know who else they were involved with and when that was, but perhaps in the late 60s. They were part of the originators who got an ambulance, an old ambulance, and that's how it started, being involved and doing good.

"They were also pretty active in the Catholic Church. That's why there were so many kids! The older boys became altar boys. My mother was very, very happy, and we wanted to please her, and that was one way to please her, by becoming an altar boy.

"It wasn't till I was in college that I had a desire to be close where things were being done and decided and I wanted to become a part of that. And in my junior year in college there were the Presidential elections and we all gathered in somebody's house and how excited I was watching how it all played out:1968, when Nixon ran. We had pizza and beer.

"Later in life, I was president of the Jaycees chapter here. In 1979, there was an opening on the Planning Board of New Paltz. We had started our business in '73 (Viking Industries) and Carol Roper, who was then the chair of the planning board, approached me about getting on the planning board, so I did and I was only there for a year or less and that led the chairman of the
New Paltz Republican Party to ask me to run for town councilman. That's when I ran against my father-in-law. I topped two other guys, too.

"That was pretty exciting: I went door-to-door, and the most exciting moment was election night when you waited for returns. We all went down to Dominic's to watch the returns coming in.

"Of course, there's always that thrill of winning. That's really some high, you know! I did that for four years. I didn't run again.

"To me, being elected as an official isn't about a career. It's being a citizen, a good citizen, doing your turn, doing your share, doing your best for that period of time and then getting out. It doesn't make sense, even today, for people to stay as long as they do. There should be term limits for **every** position. I heard somebody say that there are term limits: It's called an 'election.' It's not true, because of gerrymandering. Every party in power sets up voting districts so that their party controls the majority.

"Then as a campaign manager, I was fortunate in that all of the candidates I helped were honorable, respectable people. Actually, I would not have worked on their campaigns if I did not believe in their values and integrity. The last campaign was particularly challenging. The candidate started late in the cycle. I didn't know much about her. I was brought in late to help. Money was an issue and the committee was large, and a few members were somewhat unruly. But the candidate made up for all of that. She was the hardest working candidate whose campaign I was involved in, and when we agreed on a plan, she followed it, without complaining. The results were close, and to this day I believe her hard work and positive attitude made all the difference. It was my favorite (winning) campaign.

"My gratification, besides winning, is the fact in knowing that the people I've worked for as campaign manager are compassionately contributing to the betterment of all the citizens of our county and district. There is no better feeling and no greater reward. It's my way of giving back to the community. It all stems from that part of growing up in a group, our family, with many people who were given a sense of responsibility, accountability, and if you're not there to do your job, and you were the table setter, and you weren't there at 5 o'clock to set the table, it's like everything comes to a halt. Somebody has to pitch in and substitute, so you had to make sure you were there, 'cause the group depended on you. That was the biggest lesson. It was a responsibility to others. That's what really happens."
-Richard Croce, former Ulster County, NY legislator, town council, New Paltz, NY, and campaign manager

Richard Mathews: "When I got out of the Legislature, I was interviewed and asked what was the most rewarding thing you got out of the Legislature, and I said, 'when you get somebody who comes into your office who is lost in the maze of government, whatever level it is: city, town, county, congressional district, state, country, and you make one call and solve that problem for that person, that's great and gratifying! It's like 'Cheers;' everybody knows your name and whom to go to when you're the chairman.

"I had two things I've told my children: Be prepared when something comes and don't be afraid to take it. And I used to say, "'Little steps on ice, little steps on ice.'"
-*Richard Mathews, county chairman, board of legislators, Ulster County, NY, (retired)*

Christopher D. Petsas: "We have an obligation to help society and to help those who can't help themselves that we help rise people up with whatever mechanisms with which to do it, whether it be our physical resources or financial resources. It is our obligation to help those who cannot help themselves, our obligation to help everybody rise together and just make the world a better place for all of us. I don't care if they're Republican, I don't care if they're Democrat, I don't care what their lifestyle choices are, I don't care if they make a million dollars or not.

"It's when they call me and they say, 'Chris, I have a problem with this or that,' I don't look at my voter registry to see whether they're Republican or Democrat or any party. I don't ask those questions. I just go there and deal with the issues at hand and do everything I can to solve them. That's the way all politics should work. It doesn't work that way a lot of the time, but that's the only way I operate.

"Gay, black, straight, Latinos, I don't care what you are, as long as you're not mean-spirited, as long as you're a decent human being, my obligation as a public servant is to do my best to serve you, to help you in giving you the tools to better your life. That's the way I live."
-Christopher D. Petsas, chairman, common council, Poughkeepsie, NY

Kathleen LaBuda: "I never wanted to be involved in politics. My kids were grown and I've been involved with the Red Cross and The Federation of The Homeless and organizations associated with my church. Someone called me 'The Poster Child for all the Charitable functions.' I had a connection in that regard. I was also known as the judge's wife.

"I was homeless when I was a child. My father was a self-employed mason and a functioning alcoholic. My parents were divorced when I was in kindergarten and friends and neighbors took me in.

"I was saved by many families. My mother also used to drink as well and she was at the bars from 3 to 11 every day, working as a bartender. She was never home. My oldest brother tried to raise us, I was the sixth of seven children. As a result, I always wanted to give back and that's why I'm so involved with The Federation of The Homeless and in politics.

"People asked and commented on my concern for orphans and why I'm so involved and I would tell them 'You have no idea who I am and where I've come from, ever!'

"Both grandparents were immigrants and my father was a hard worker, but come Friday night and payday, he headed right to the bars and most times, we didn't see him again till Sunday. That was a ritual.

"I was fifteen when we moved to Sullivan County. My mother moved us every two years. Very hard on me because of my loss of friends. She had gotten another divorce and circumstances made us move, not paying rent, trying to forge checks for food, everything.

"When we were kids, we needed food and The Salvation Army gave my mother a box of cereal, a block of cheese, a five pound bag of potatoes and powdered milk until she got her food stamps. We also got our Christmas toys from The Salvation Army. People have no idea.

"When I was a kid, five or six, my mother swept floors in a beauty shop and I went to get the bagels and coffee for people. I was 'the Bagel Kid." Later on, I used to iron clothes for money, babysit, clean houses, etc. When I lived here, I worked at The Concord (Hotel).

I made a fortune and that's how I put myself through college. I worked in the coffee shop. I was a waitress. I worked a hospital switchboard at night. I did multiple jobs. There wasn't a job too big or too small that I wouldn't do to make money.

"I attended OCCC and took prerequisite classes for nursing. While my children were young, I then went back to SCCC several years later to finish my nursing degree. During that time, my husband, Frank, was sent to Desert Storm in 1990, and 1991. Upon his return, I became pregnant with my daughter, Erika. I developed toxemia and was on bed rest, which meant I had to drop out of college. I had lost a daughter years earlier. So I had to be extremely careful.

"I never look back and I believe that things happen for a reason.

"One woman in one of the neighboring towns had no groceries and they were about to turn off her lights. In the social service system, 80% of those people needed help and money. You can't believe how people with a couple of kids are trying to make ends meet. I bought groceries for her. I didn't tell anybody. Stuff like that. I did it all the time. People are desperate and need those services and need that money.

"I'm a survivor. Do you know how many people have come to me and said 'Thank you so much for helping me'? Everything I do is with a purpose.

"It was through my own personal experiences that I believe I became a successful county legislator, dedicated to helping others. I didn't want other people to go through what I had to as a child.

"I tell my daughter Erika these stories and they're all true! Now **SHE** helps children in other parts of the world, particularly when visiting South Africa at a particular orphanage."

"It is my own strong faith that I had been able to get through this and help spare others who have found themselves in similar situations. A painting of St. Theresa is at the entrance of my home and I pray to her on a daily basis, and she inspires me every day."
-Kathleen LaBuda, county legislator, Sullivan County, NY

Frank L. Cardinale: "When I was in college, I got involved with the protest movements, marched, and when I got out of college, I realized there's more to life than making as much money as you can. Although the reality does hit you in the face later on when you have to do that and when you have your own family and kids to send to college. But there's more to it than that and coming back and working on Frank Koenig's mayoral campaign (in Kingston, NY) changed me. It really did.

"When I got out of college, I was working as a field engineer for a group of insurance companies in New England. Mr. Koenig (now deceased), a family friend, ran and became mayor of Kingston. He would've loved Mike Hein (Ulster County executive). They are of the same mold. He was the consummate mayor, the local guy whom everybody loved, and as close to a professional as you'd find in politics. He was the best mayor this city has ever had: Very conscientious, a bit conservative, a fiscal conservative. Today, if you're not fiscally responsible, there's something wrong with you.

"And so, he asked me, 'What are ya doing? What are ya doing tonight?"
I need young people to work in my campaign.'

"I said, 'Nothing. I'll go help.' So I got involved in that campaign and I liked it. I learned a lot. They had an insurance office on Broadway and it was a hotbed: all kinds of activities, all kinds of stuff going on. Frank said, 'I need you to go to this house. I need this. I need you to go to that house.' And he won handily because the campaign was so tight. I always use that as a backdrop, meaning well-organized, extremely well-organized.

"It isn't much different today of how to run a campaign than politics was back then. People have changed a little bit, but the methods haven't. It's easier now, but back then, everything was manual. They didn't have computers. They didn't have anything to help them print out walking lists. They had to do everything manually. So it was difficult, but that's what got me involved.

"There is no ideology involved in local politics, nothing substantial. It's all about: We have an infrastructure project we need to get done. How can we do it most effectively and efficiently? And if you go to town board meetings, most of them are operated that way. If you look at them, you wouldn't know who is a Democrat or Republican if you didn't know them. That's what I love about town politics and that's why it's so important that you get good people at any level, and when you get good people at the town level, it lifts everybody up.

"Now we have some good people we can try to interest in running for higher office, and that's part of the 'building the bench.'

"I really wanted to contribute something for the community, so I'm all over the place now. You do the job that's the best that you can and say to yourself, 'What do I have to lose? A salary and benefits? Oh, that's right, I don't have any salary and benefits.' And if you keep that mindset, it's actually cost me a lot of money. It's a voluntary job.

"I go to state conventions, have to stay over, driving expenses, all out of my own pocket. I go to other campaign events. I buy tickets just like everybody else does, but I have to go to more than most people do. I'm not complaining; I can leave tomorrow if I want. That's not the issue.

"I like what I'm doing so long as I think I'm making headway and inroads for the county and that things are going well."
- *Frank L. Cardinale, chairman, Democratic Party, Ulster County, NY*

Mark Sherman: "The best legacy of all is the fact that you can make a difference in a small community. In a small town there's no excuse for not speaking your mind. My legacy would be for my children and their children knowing that you can make a difference and won't say, 'What the heck, I can't change things,' because *I* know you can.

"Senator Teddy Kennedy, during his eulogy for his brother, Senator Robert F. Kennedy, said, 'Some men see things as they are and say, 'Why?' 'I dream of things that never were and say, 'Why not?'

"Those words are profound. If you take it to an extreme, you get people like Martin Luther King, Jr. who say it doesn't have to be this way. And, of course, at that level you talk about courage, and that's major-- courage. Maybe not so much in small towns, but when you go beyond that, you can see the risk they're taking. But they are the people who've changed the world."
-*Mark Sherman, former town councilman, New Paltz, NY*

I told Mr. Sherman that 'He was one of them, as well.'

Diana Spada: "The sense of helping people came from my grandmother and grandfather and my mother. I don't ever remember a time that my grandmother and grandfather or mother weren't helping someone. We had a restaurant and the employees were like family. We were closed on Sunday and they were at our house eating dinner with us. When we were catering and there was extra food left over, the employees took it home. I also had to give to others going to Catholic School, quite honestly.

That was something that we had to do in school. We had to do something of community service. It was just required all throughout high school. It was just something that was always there.

"Nothing was ever talked about in my family life that didn't include politics. Any conversation always comes to politics. 'It's raining out. Wow, it's raining because it's Election Day and when it rains, it keeps the Republicans home and the Democrats vote.' I mean it doesn't matter. That's just the way it is. Sunday mornings were always with my great grandparents watching '"Meet the Press."' So it was just ingrained in me.

"I grew up with politics. I grew up hearing both sides, and there's validity on both sides. I'm in the middle. Politics is the necessary evil to do good. You have to go through that process to be able to effectuate change and to do good and help people.

"I really, truly believe that people do it for the right reasons, the right people do it for the right reasons and I learned that the hard way, and I learned that there's a difference between the definition of politics and a person in politics.

"My commitment (as a campaign manager/strategist) is to the candidate, not the husbands, wives, mothers, aunts, uncles, friends or political allies or other elected officials. It's the candidate I'm working with.

Diana Spada's assistant campaign strategist "Flint"

"I tend to lean toward the law and order. I like the judicial. I love federal politics, federal races. I love senatorial races, congressional races, presidential races. On the federal level, the presidency has always been a fascination of mine. I used to tell my grandfather, ever since I was a little girl that I was going to be the first female p––resident and he'd look at me and say, 'If there's going to be anyone, it's going to be *YOU!*"
-Diana Spada, campaign strategist, Kingston, NY

Susan Zimet: "At the end of the day, yes, politics is important, but people forget it really isn't about politics, it is about public service. When you are fortunate to serve in an elected capacity and do good things for your community, being able to help people in your capacity, it is a great privilege and a great honor, but it's not the end all, be all.

'Ultimately, it's the people you surround yourself with that matters. It determines who you are and what you believe in. It is how you live your life and how you treat others that matters. And ultimately, the truth always comes out. It does.

"When I was asked what is it about getting into politics and serving the public, I responded with one word– Passion. The night I got elected, a woman came over to me and said, 'Thank you for what you did for every girl in New Paltz.' Then, when I was supervisor, I used to go to the classrooms and have a lot of meetings with the kids, and got lots of thank you notes and cards from young girls about inspiring them. Children are my passion."

Ms. Zimet: "My dream was to be the first woman in professional baseball. That was my dream. It didn't happen, but I was elected as the first woman Supervisor of the Town of New Paltz and was able to inspire young girls. At opening day of the New Paltz Youth baseball season, I would talk about my dream to become the first woman in baseball. I would say, that decades later, no woman has yet to break the baseball glass ceiling! But I do stand here before you, the first woman supervisor of the Town of New Paltz!"

Steve Auerbach, Susan Zimet's husband and campaign manager: **"Susan loved being able to get involved**, to do things and make things happen and make life better for people. That was the aspect of her job she loved. When I was raised, my parents, who were holocaust survivors, didn't have any money, but we were always expected to give back to others. That's the way **we** grew up."
-Susan Zimet, former town supervisor, New Paltz, NY and county legislator, Ulster County, NY
and Steven Auerbach, campaign manager

Anthony McGinty: "For me, I've been able to communicate by telling stories about issues in Family Court from cases I've adjudicated. No names, of course. I relate how I think about these cases and how I participated in some way in getting families through a difficult part of their lives and moving toward a healthy and happy family situation. You want to connect emotionally with people, and the way to do this is to tell stories about people you've known or met or connected with."

Sara McGinty adds: " You have to be a lawyer with your head and your heart, and a judge has to be the same way."
-Anthony McGinty, family court judge, Ulster County, NY and
Sara McGinty, surrogate's court judge for Ulster County, NY, attorney and former town judge, Rosendale, NY,

CHAPTER 1
THE ETERNAL QUEST FOR VICTORY

"Victory has a thousand fathers, defeat is an orphan."
-President John F. Kennedy

IT MATTERS NOT TO ME whether you're a member of the Democrat, Republican, Independent, Conservative, Green, Tea, Rainbow, Blue Enigma, Purple, Orange, Gray, Whatever Color, Left Wing, Right Wing, Chicken Wing, Constitution, Libertarian, Cocktail, Working Families, Public Servant, Union Member, Organization Member, Corporate Exec, Club, Group, Student Council, Women, Men, Straight, Gay, Bi-, Transgender, Alliance, Bull Moose, Rent Is Too Damn High Party.

I AM GOING TO HELP YOU, no matter who you are, what party or organization you belong to, or how inexperienced – or experienced – you may be.

I cannot, of course, guarantee a win for you. Nothing in life is guaranteed, but I am going to improve your chances enormously in your quest for **VICTORY** with ideas and critically important suggestions. I will infinitely improve your chances for electoral **SUCCESS**, and hopefully, as well, by an overwhelming landslide.

This book will give you the practical, realistic basics of campaigning and will provide you with an insight into the human nature and rationale of subjecting one's self to the rigors and strategy of successful campaigning. There are lots of other books and websites on the market with an incredible amount of encyclopedic information, and I encourage you to research and use them, but this one gets right to the heart, emotion and behavior expected of candidates and incumbents.

It is sometimes very raw, but that's life, especially when one has to play hardball, whether in the majors or on local farm teams. You will acquire information here never written about elsewhere. I've interviewed politicians/public servants from both sides of the aisle to acquire the nuanced information to follow. Politics in any election and situation, in any locale, in any union, school or sales force, is emotional and competitive.

> *"Running for office is like standing in the middle of the street, naked and vulnerable."*
> -Elliott Auerbach, comptroller, Ulster County, NY

WINNING IS EVERYTHING. Don't let anyone fool you into thinking otherwise. This book was not written for losers. You have to go after your opponent without mercy. You'll feel terrific in doing so and in knowing you've put your all into this power-hungry, (hopefully) "do-good" endeavor. I only hope you can keep it as clean and honest as possible and beat the living… turkey stuffing out of your opponents at the same time.

"I think it's important to highlight the fact that there are many different paths to winning an election. We see that time and time again. The reality is, we've chosen one that is very, very specific and that is one built on integrity. This is important to me personally and we continually have taken the high road. That is not a simple thing to do in this day and age, but negative campaigning is not a path I have chosen. I believe you can do the right thing, work hard, and highlight a record that is beneficial to the citizens that you represent if you embrace with honor the duty and responsibility that is necessary to earn the public's trust."
-Michael P. Hein, county executive, Ulster County, NY

Here's a tribute from the chair of the Ulster County, NY, Democratic Party to the county executive. I use it as an example of the respect from one dedicated public servant to another, and of the personal testimonial to one who has given so much to the county. It has nothing to do with the selection of one's party. The reward for public servants is the satisfaction of bettering the community for everyone.
"There's a difference between being an executive and in an elected office, being in the legislative branch vs. being an executive. Mike (Hein, Ulster County executive) is a doer. He needs to get things done. He'd be stifled in congress. I told him I'd support him no matter what he decided to do. He has earned my support. He's that good. In my lifetime, I've never seen anybody turn around a county like he has, in every respect. If you don't like him personally, I don't really care. This guy has done a remarkable job here."
-Frank Cardinale, chairman, Democratic Party, Ulster County, NY,

"Winners have an inner conviction that they can go forth and change the world- they have a really deep need to change things. They have to do this, they think. They have no choice. But you really have to have a thick skin, because if they find a soft spot, they'll eat you alive.

"It's the inner drive within you that can make a difference. Relating to tennis: You take your lessons, plan strategy, develop your technique, but you're going to crumble if you're down six love and you're not mentally strong enough to hang in there, no matter how much you've trained. Lack of resolve will defeat a good athlete, but the winners are the ones who fight back and never give up. You have to have conviction, energy and a real belief you can win."
-Marcy Goulart, former president, Democratic Women of Ulster County, NY

From a fortune cookie

CHAPTER 2
EGO, POWER AND PASSION

"You were born to win, but to be a winner, you must plan to win, prepare to win, and expect to win."
-Zig Ziglar, motivational speaker and author

The Political Personality: The driving, churning river of power flows uncontrollably until it is harnessed to create electric energy. It moves boulders and trees and changes the shoreline and unless dammed, it moves unabated. It's the lifeblood of endless communities and their destruction, as well, when it overflows.

It's the political personality that hungers for power, loves the game, loves the rough and tumble of shooting the rapids, moving great boulders out of the way and creating electricity capable of moving mountains.

It's backslapping, pressing the flesh, hugging, kissing, schmoozing, finessing, cajoling, manipulating, strategizing, convincing, planning, warring, pacifying, reasoning, compromising and give and take, if necessary. It's the political game and those who play it better, win most often. It's relentless. It's the quest for political power. However small the election, however rural the community, it's always about winning the "Super Bowl."

It's the love of combat with adversaries, and that's what a political personality is all about. It's the aura and rush of power that flows like a river to incumbents, the power to make decisions that affect other people's lives, and all the attention and perks one receives while on the throne.

"We're just a speck of sand on the beach of the history of Saugerties and while we're here, we should do what's best for the town and/or village. Period."
-*Greg Helsmoortel, town supervisor, Saugerties, NY*

First Things First:
Who put YOU up to run for office: Yourself or people you work with, political party campaign committee members, business associates from work or local organizations, golf partners, fellow party or union members, sales associates or fellow students? If they suggest you run and interview you, can you make a compelling argument why YOU should be selected?

Chairman Frank Cardinale of the Ulster County, NY, Democratic Party says, "The first thing, of course, is getting the best candidates that you can find. There's no substitute for a good candidate. **Trying to prop up a bad candidate is bad 'business.' In some cases, when picking a bad candidate, you lose credibility.** You don't wait till the last moment. You try to identify people and, if you've lived here long enough, you get to know people: town board members that have an interest in running for higher office."

Are you comfortable and able to outline the reasons you are truly the right person at the right time for a political office? Did you have an epiphany moment, as did Dan Torres, deputy Town of New Paltz supervisor and assistant county comptroller, who simply had to be involved in making things better in his community?

Are you more of an "advise and consent" collaborator? Do you have the background for detailed legislative lawmaking? Are you a decisive, confident, decision-maker who is driven by the adrenaline of day-to-day pressure decision-making? Are you able to assume executive power and lead the troops when everything is at stake? How would you handle the Flint, Michigan, water poisoning crisis and do you see yourself dropping everything to ensure the health and safety of the citizens you're sworn to represent and protect?

Mr. Cardinale stated, "There are people in the legislature that if you didn't know who they were, you wouldn't know who they were. I know 'cause I'm in politics, but they don't do anything, they don't make any major contributions, they just vote on party line. That party wants to select people they think who can just win, and once they get there, well, we have three or four people who can guide them through to get the items passed. And they do. We had a couple like that, two or three who are totally 'off the reservation' and so that's what happens. It's a popularity contest on the local level, too."

Your responsibilities in smaller communities may be proportionately less, but health, safety, stability, well-being and a myriad of meat and potatoes issues are daily occurrences. If you think you can deal with all of that, then, by all means, run for office.

"**Luck is when opportunity intersects with preparation.** I studied all the local issues. How? By reading every local newspaper religiously, which I do to this day, speaking with those people whom I met, often on a one-on-one basis, to familiarize myself with local problems and then take stands that I thought would be of benefit to the people. It's really exciting. Everything else becomes secondary. What you do on a daily basis to make government work or 'oil the machinery,' so to speak, is really secondary to the human side of public service."
-Elliott Auerbach, comptroller, Ulster County, NY

Because if you think you may not be up to those challenges of serving the citizenry of your communities or states or country, do step aside.
They all "cut to the core of who you are as an individual," states Ulster County Executive, **Michael P. Hein**. You have to believe that a well-run government can benefit everyone and your participation as a reformer will mean the difference for people living in comfort or in daily anger, fear and anxiety.

If you're thinking of running, think of the legacy you'll leave behind; heroic in stature or billy goat? It will reflect on your family, as well.

EGO and POWER: If you don't have the strongest ego and constitution, you'll be crushed. You can't have a glass jaw because, if you do, you're going to be counted out by an opponent who cannot wait to beat the hell out of you. You have to put up your dukes at all times and keep a clear idea of why you're running, and ignore, as much as possible, what the press is writing. It's not over till the last bell rings at the end of the bout.

You have to fight for every round and if you're knocked down, get yourself up and keep going and, with your campaign manager's help, wait till the right moment and then land that uppercut to knock your opponent out. (I'll leave the left and right hooks out of this.)

"My dad always said, 'Champ, the measure of a man is not how often he is knocked down, but how quickly he gets up.'"
-Joe Biden, vice-president of the United States

And you have to stand your ground regarding all the things people think you should be doing. Listen politely, but only go in the direction in which you're most comfortable. You need people you trust implicitly to give you realistic, unbiased opinions. Speak with conviction and don't shoot yourself in the foot with spur of the moment ideas that haven't been strategized and completely thought out. Before loose-lipping it, rip that loose tongue out.

Attend every event and relentlessly convey your winning qualities. You have to stand in the middle of the ring and **earn their votes**, day after day, night after night at diners, bars, chicken barbecues, dinners, meatball and spaghetti extravagandas and country fairs, trying to convince people why you deserve their support, both by their vote and by their financial contributions.

As for chicken dinners, there's a wise old Yiddish expression, which applies to not doing everything you can to win a campaign, "You can't make chicken soup out of chicken shit."

You HAVE to be the winner, and must decide that you're the man or woman who will make a real difference in people's lives. Charisma is absolutely a factor in one's appeal, but you have to have that inner drive and stamina to work tirelessly, which might be even more important, ultimately, than just a charismatic appearance. Make the best chicken soup.

If your ego isn't strong enough and you don't have the confidence in yourself, it will come across to people. They will sense your poor speech projection and weak body language. Those two subtle factors make a huge negative impression. Take a look at the candidates running for President and analyze why some appear so much stronger than others, whether you agree with them or not. It's interesting, that Hillary Clinton, in one of her debates, recognized that she wasn't a natural politician like her husband and Barack Obama, and that she had to work harder to convince people of what she believed in.

Rich Mathews said, **"You can't ever forget where you've come from."** Successful candidates who have a better chance in local elections are those who were born and raised in their communities, whose roots are well established in the community and whose parents, siblings, their parents, grandparents, great grandparents and cousins have lived there for generations. They might be in a family business or profession or practice, and those candidates would be the perfect people to run for office, not a "carpetbagger" who claims residence just for the sake of eligibility to run for elected office. **"Carpetbagger"** is a powerful negative image for a candidate to overcome. "Who the hell does he think he is, coming in here and thinking he's gonna buy that election?" We've all heard that many times before.

In Judge Anthony T. Kane's case, he ran a grassroots campaign. "I had no money, but I was established in the community and not considered to be a 'carpetbagger.' People in the Town of Thompson knew me in Fallsburg and Mamakating, and I had been in the Army Reserves. That introduced me to roughly 120 other young men from Sullivan County. It was a great way to have been introduced into the community, and… I get along with most people."

He and his wife, Nancy, then started going to events and saying hello to people. In local communities, those are church breakfasts, fire company breakfasts and lots of those chicken barbecues. That's where they got a great deal of positive feedback.

"Now the general who wins a battle makes many calculations in his temple ere the battle is fought. The general who loses a battle makes but few calculations beforehand. Thus do many calculations lead to victory, and few calculations to defeat: how much more no calculation at all! It is by attention to this point that I can foresee who is likely to win or lose."
-Sun Tzu, *The Art of War*

WHY YOU? WHY RUN?

You think you're special, but ask yourself why they want you specifically. Why should they vote for you instead of the opposing candidate(s)? Are you perceived to be a winner, a puppet for their agenda, or sacrificial lamb? Where do you fit in, and if you're going to be their puppet or lamb, do you really want to put yourself in that demeaning position?

PASSION: Do you think you have the brains, related experience, education, passion, nerve and leadership qualities in both military and civilian life, to handle the enormous responsibilities of elected office, whatever they may be? Are you angry about current conditions and a perception you have of non-responsive government? You must not deceive yourself from the outset and simply not waste their time nor yours.

"In my lifetime, when I've been underestimated, I actually performed better. Really, throughout all my life, it always put me in a stronger place, so it actually helped me."
-Congressman Chris Gibson, House of Representatives, 19th district, NY

"When I got out of the Legislature, I was interviewed and asked what was the most rewarding thing you got out of the Legislature, and I said, 'When you get somebody who comes into your office who is lost in the maze of government, whatever level it is: city, town, county, congressional district, state, country, and you make one call and solve that problem for that person, that's great and gratifying! It's like 'Cheers;' everybody knows your name when you're the *chairman*."
-Richard Mathews- retired county chairman, Ulster County, NY.

And that's what it's all about for public servants who give it their all.

Look in The Mirror: What are your attributes and involvement in the community? Did you grow up in your community? What are your strengths and weaknesses? Do you have the background to run for your desired particular office? Do you have the backbone to withstand the opposition? Compare your strengths and weaknesses. Do you think you can overcome your weaknesses against strong opponents?

If not, and you win, do you want to be eaten alive by people more capable than you? Do you want to be someone's poodle and have them pull your leash, or do you want to keep your head held high? Do you have an outsized personality to make people want to support you?

Be a candidate for all the right reasons and "This above all; to thine own self, be true."
-William Shakespeare, *Hamlet*

CHAPTER 3
The "Come to Jesus Moment"

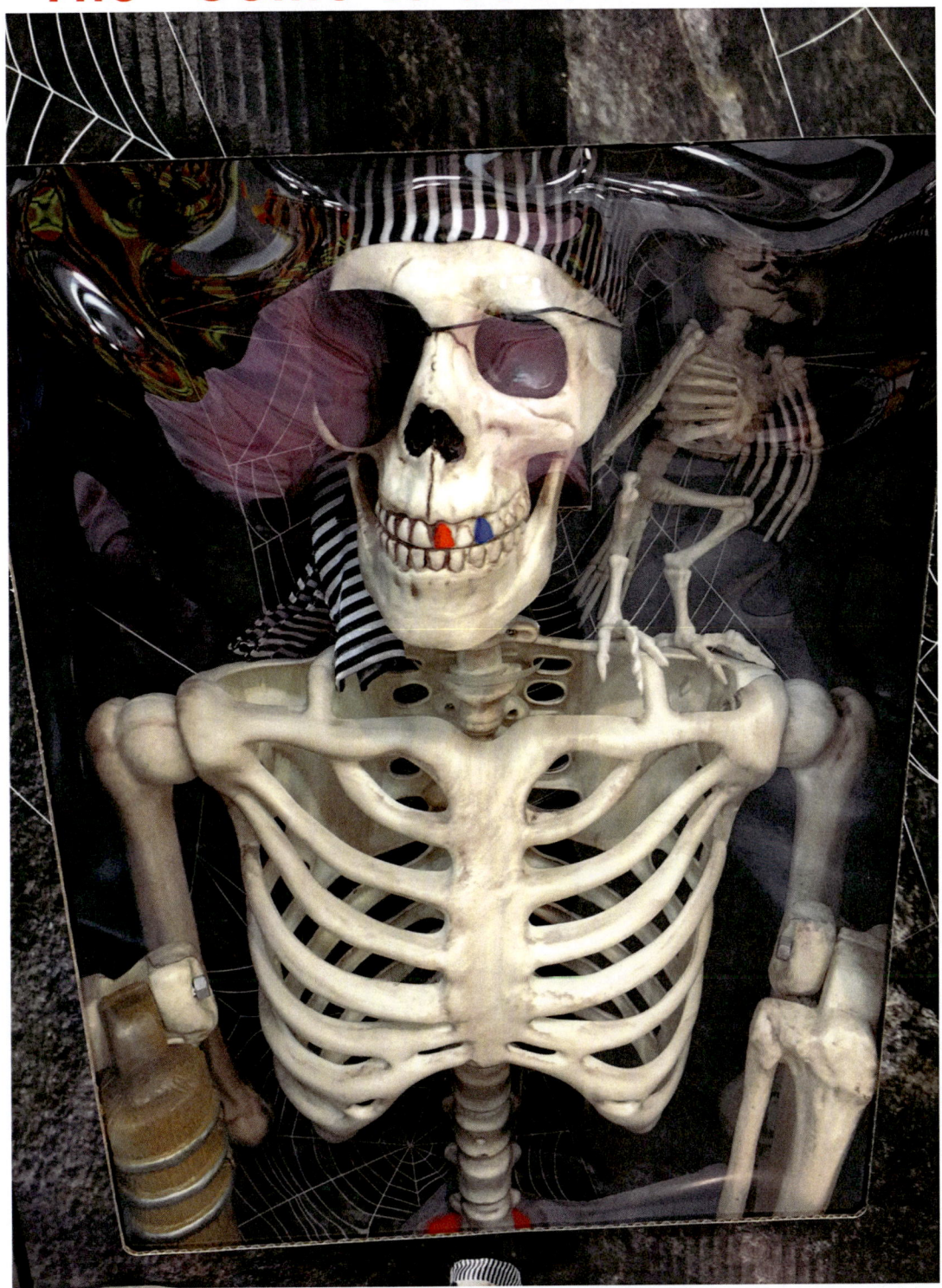

Any skeletons in your closet?

What skeletons do you have in your closet? You **MUST** reveal anything detrimental about yourself to your campaign strategist and/or campaign manager beforehand. If those skeletons appear when that closet door is opened and you haven't revealed them, you are totally blindsiding the people you will need the most.

Campaign strategist Diana Spada, calls it the "Come to Jesus Moment." She says, "You don't walk on water, you're not Jesus, we're all human and we all make mistakes." She needs to know everything about a potential candidate's background and skeletons before considering working for potential candidates. You have to be absolutely candid. Your information will always stay with your strategists. If you have a skeleton, your opposition will find it. There are many strategists for the opposition who, like Ms. Spada, revel in opposition research. She is very tough on potential candidates, as well one should be. She wants to know the very worst thing about you and states that she cannot help a candidate unless all is revealed.

In smaller, local campaigns, many campaign managers and strategists volunteer their time and political expertise. They believe in their candidates and they spend an enormous amount of time in trying to get their candidates elected, and so those candidates must be vetted as carefully as if they were running for president.

Building a Bench: Mr. Cardinale, when he was appointed as chairman of the Ulster County Democratic Party, felt that it was imperative to find good people who wanted to run for various offices at the local level, such as town council and town supervisor; people who had a desire to participate in government. Finding the best people is called "building a bench."

He said, "Now we have some good people we can try to interest in running for higher office, and that's part of the 'building the bench.' We continue to replenish, and we're doing a great job, we really are, in towns where they've been Republican strongholds, and we're beginning to turn the corner in a lot of the towns.

"Most of the people who are getting involved in politics are professionals or even semi-retired professionals in some fields: nursing, business, other fields, etc. In the past four years, we have been developing that 'bench' of people.

"What I do is go back and try to tap into the various town board members. You don't want to lose them at that level, but you don't necessarily lose them. They might consider running for the legislature as well, and once you're in the legislature, at some point of time, and you never know when, there might be an assembly position available. We do have four assembly districts and four senate districts in this county, but they may be good enough to want to run for even higher office.

"But you never really know until they get active. They'll build confidence. They'll feel like they're making a contribution and they'll feel good about it, and they want to do more. It kinda gets in your blood. It really does."

Questions a campaign manager should first ask: If you are considering the campaign manager's position, whether paid or voluntary, here are some critical questions to ask the candidate before you make a final decision:

- Will you "buy" into my campaign strategy?
- Will you commit to personally knocking on doors?
- Do you have any volunteers willing to give you their time, money and enthusiasm?
- Do you have any money to run a campaign?
- How much money do you have to spend on the campaign?
- Can you raise more money from family and contacts?

Strategists and opposition researchers love to rub their hands together and dig and dig and dig until they find something on you. Ever watch a dog dig a hole and observe all the dirt flying into the air behind it? That's what opposition researchers love to do. They love to make that dirt fly. They'll dig into your financials, dig into taxes not paid, newspapers, magazines, past public comments you've made publically on various issues, scandals, juicy sexcapades, votes cast as well as controversial organizations and people with whom you've been associated. And when they find something on you, you will be hung out to dry, or perhaps, twist in the wind in embarrassment. In this day and age, news travels at warp speed and you could find yourself thrown into a black hole, unable to emerge, and you will be the laughingstock of your community. In other words, come clean beforehand.

If you hold anything back, it will be devastating for you and all the people who would be working on your behalf. Oh, and by the way, and more likely than not, you will severely jeopardize your chances for winning. Kiss your election goodbye when your opponents smell blood and attack.

The sharks are in the water circling your boat and given the opportunity, they'll be all over you, and then eat you alive.

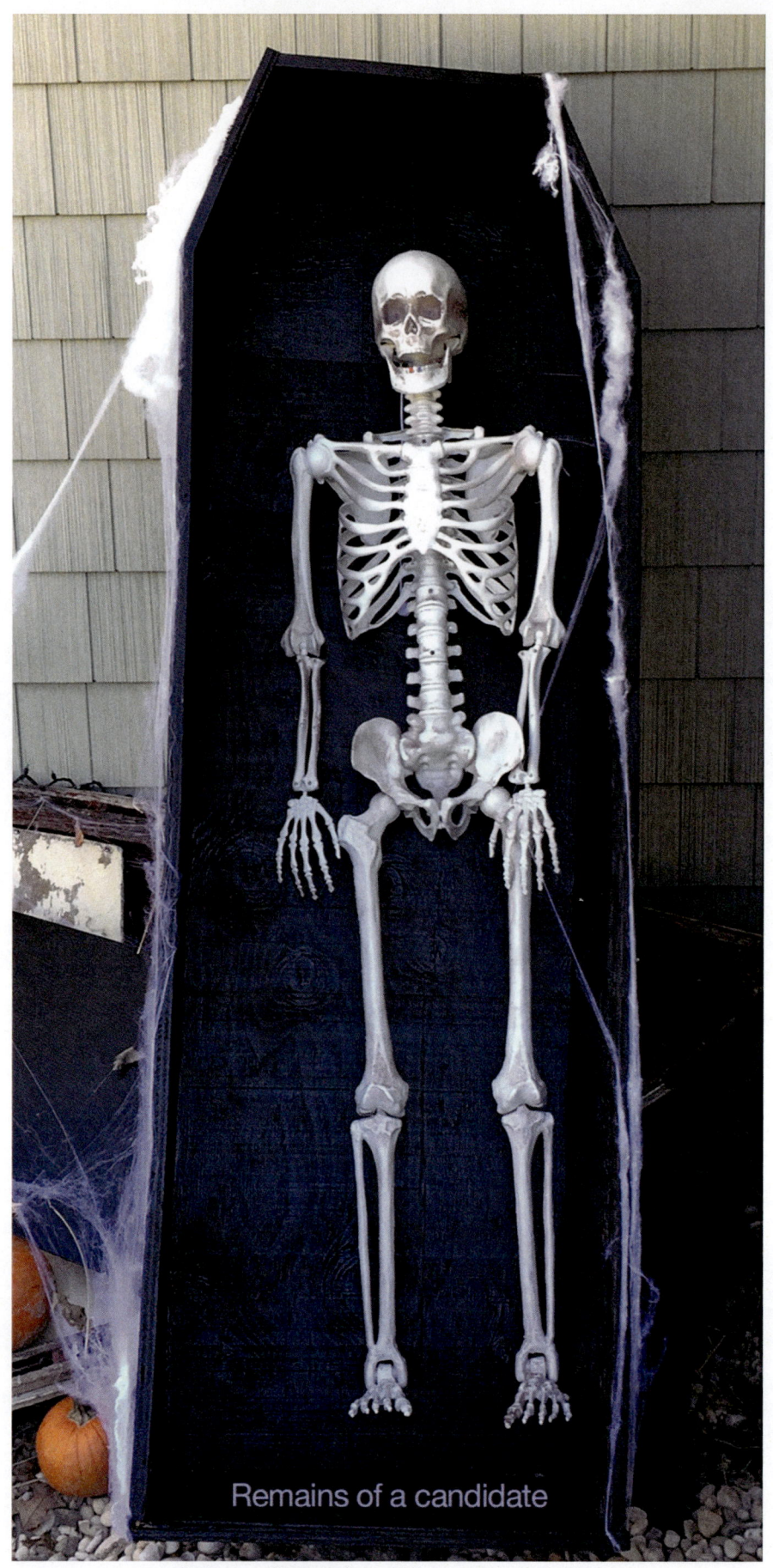

All that will be left...will be your skeleton.

So "Come to Jesus," and don't give your opponents the opportunity of creating questions regarding your character and integrity. Voters will respect your candidness and respect that you were man or woman enough to admit your mistakes. America is a very forgiving nation. We don't tolerate liars, but we do open our hearts to candidates who have recognized their wrong doings in public forums.

Are You a Giver or a Taker? Make a list of reasons why you want to run: altruistic desire to help serve people in the community or organization? Power, steady salary, health insurance, retirement plan, patriotic desire to help the country, fame, potential kickbacks filling your pockets? Promises of a job after serving? Anger? Frustration? Destiny, a calling influenced by your religious beliefs?

Kathleen LaBuda of Wurtsboro, NY, was asked by a couple of local politicians to become a candidate for the Sullivan County Legislature. She said she didn't want to get involved in politics, but they felt that she had done so much for the community as chairlady of the local Red Cross chapter, director of the Federation for The Homeless and president of The Ladies Auxiliary of the American Legion, that they convinced her to jump into the pool, not quite knowing how to swim.

Her husband referred her to a local advertising executive and political strategist, **Bernard Cohen**, of Monticello, NY, who asked her the "Come to Jesus" (maybe Moses, in his case) question after she told him she thought she could make a difference.

"Tell me how," he said.

"I have the background and knowledge of various organizations. I'm familiar with Sullivan County and I think I can do a good job because of my community volunteering experience." That satisfied Mr. Cohen enough for him to refer her to one of the local well-connected political ladies in the area, with whom she met at a diner over lunch to see whether she thought "I could win or not." Ms. LaBuda was then told she *had* to run.

The lady said, "We love your husband. I'll arrange a fundraiser for you and whatever else you want."

Mr. Cohen agreed to work on Ms. LaBuda's campaign and strategized with her, telling her she had to establish herself, and he was one of the forces behind her. They got volunteers on board who worked extremely hard for her to help determine the most important local issues of local concern. Mr. Cohen did all the public relations, fliers and letters through his printing/advertising agency.

She was a Democrat in a heavily Republican county, by 2 to 1, but they felt the incumbent was vulnerable. Ms. LaBuda interviewed numerous residents and noted every complaint on her pad and reported back to Mr. Cohen. "I'd ask what their biggest concern was and what would you want your legislator to change?" They then came up with the three or four most important issues for her platform. Of course, everyone's biggest beefs were property taxes, then antiquated cell service for the firemen and a lack of public transportation in rural areas for seniors and other citizens to get to the shopping centers.

Ms. LaBuda launched a vigorous campaign, going to all the functions, fundraisers and chicken barbecues, wherever the most people were expected to attend. She always tried to have one of the leading ladies in the Party introduce her. "I want you to meet Kathy LaBuda who is running for the County Legislature and we hope you can support her. She's been a great person for the community" and they mentioned all her organizations with which she was involved.

Someone called her "The poster child for all the charitable organizations." She was also known as the judge's wife. That connection was also a great asset. She felt it was tremendously important to have somebody who's well-liked in the community to take her around, as well as meeting with the chairmen of each township to ask for their help.

"The motivating factor was to live in a better community, as opposed to moving out of it. The only way to make a change is if you're in the game. People talk about making changes or complain, but don't do anything about it, so rather than be part of the problem, I decided to be part of the solution."
-Jeff Siegel- candidate for County Legislature, Sullivan County, NY

Marcy Goulart, former pres. of Ulster County, NY, Democratic Women, says, "I don't want to support anyone who's 'kumbaya.' I want someone who will go in there and make things better. Prove every day that he or she is doing it."

Part of Frank Cardinale's job as party chair is to get the right people to represent their various communities and gain the political power to influence local government for the betterment of everyone. It all starts with local, off-year elections and getting people to realize how influential their votes are. The challenge and strategy is to try to get people to vote in local elections as often as they would in state and national elections.

He claims that school board, town and county elections generally get approximately 10% to 12% of registered voters and residents, but if they get 35% to 40%, "you'd be doing pretty good. That's why we try to influence local elections. It's the off-year elections and electing local representatives that has a bigger impact on peoples' lives, and they just don't realize it."

Do you have the party, business and public servants supporting you with their valued endorsements? Personal endorsements from fellow citizens, perhaps neighbors not politically connected, are equally important. They ground you in the publics' eye and perception. Sara McGinty, candidate for Ulster County, NY, surrogate's court, states, "that it's important to volunteer for party candidates, to be on committees, work the phone banks. It means a lot. Committee members who choose candidates want to know that you've invested in the party and its candidates, and that you respect the work that they do."

If you're running for national office, your staff members, directed by your campaign manager, if seasoned and having worked on many campaigns, will go into a district and direct their efforts toward your winning.

"I returned home after college," said Elliott Auerbach- to help out in the hardware store for a little while, at my father's request, and remained in Ellenville for the next 22 years. It was the best education one could ever have. First, I was with my wonderful parents every day, both as son and then partner. My dad taught me everything there was to know about the store. But I also learned people skills and how to talk to people and how to listen to and solve the problems they came in with.

"I tell constituents that it was in Ace Hardware that I learned to mind the store. I grew up in a service environment and that has carried over to my involvement in local government.

"The late mayor of Ellenville, a flamboyant guy named Ed Jacobs, saw something in me and nurtured my interest in local affairs, casually starting to mentor me in local politics. It was a field I had never even thought of, but Ed saw something in me from my behavior in the hardware store, and like any great teacher, he guided and encouraged me to get involved. All it takes is one person to change one's direction in life. That was Ed.

"In the years back in Ellenville, I was pissed off by government officials who lied to the people, wronged people, and hadn't done things properly; a bunch of phonies who were entrusted to run the village, excluding Mayor Ed Jacobs. I reached out to people who felt the same way, and ultimately, I was selected to run for village trustee. I ended up serving for two terms and was then elected to become mayor, and served for three terms in that position. This was long after Mayor Jacobs was no longer serving.

"One has to spend one's own human capital and reach out to friends and colleagues for support. Making friends is key. You have to relate to people, to be real. The hardware store was my textbook for communication skills. My dad and mom were my true professors."
- Elliott Auerbach, comptroller, Ulster County, NY

CHAPTER 4
THE CAMPAIGN MANAGER: A MAESTRO TO CONDUCT THE ORCHESTRA

*"There is no reward for second place.
Winner take all. You lose an election, that's it,
you lose an election.
Not a pleasant feeling.
We don't work to lose."*
-Richard Croce, campaign manager in numerous judicial and district attorney campaigns

Whether you're an incumbent or a first time candidate, you need to get the right people to help you and it's important that you create a network of people you can rely on. They can be colleagues you've worked with, business people, political people in the system, family members and trusted friends.

Chairman Cardinale says, "If you can find somebody that you know can be effective as an elected official, someone popular in the community who will do the work, you got a winner. You can't always get those three things, unfortunately, but you can work your way through a campaign even though you may not be the most popular person in the community or people don't know you.

"If you're willing to work, absolutely you can negate that deficit right up front. You can. That's local politics and what we do is we make sure that they have all the materials they need and we work with their town chairs and we try to look over the shoulders, sometimes, of a town committee. Some town committees are better than others and we know which ones are weak and which candidates need a little bit more help from us. And so we try to fill in."

The ideas that the committees will come up with help you refine your ideals and goals, and having a meal or coffee with them will informally bond the right ones with you. They're the ones who will open doors for you, who will introduce you to the power players in the community.

An effective way to campaign and raise money is to attend home parties and informal gatherings. You'll be introduced and, practicing beforehand, make a little speech. This is the same as developing a network, but on a highly personal level. Some of your supporters will contribute money. Others who may not be able to contribute money will contribute wisdom. That can be worth far more in the long run than money, and probably provide you with contacts you'd never be able to meet on your own. All of these people, you hope, will be convinced you're the right person for the job… if you do it right.

Adele Reiter stated that they want you to say, "I remember what frustrated me with government when I was on the outside, and I'm going to get that job done. That was what was important to the people who elected me, and they were right." They're looking for a candidate who will achieve their goals and who will do the job like they would do if they, themselves, were in office.

Mr. Cardinale makes the point that getting people elected is the most important thing. But "In some towns there are Republican supervisors who do a great job. My philosophy is if I can't find somebody who I feel can do a better job, than this person, and particularly if they're not political, and a lot of the supervisors aren't, and they're in it to do what they can for the town, I'll leave that person alone. I'm not going after him. And we have crossed some doors, three or four supervisors, because they do a great job and they work across the aisle. They all work mostly together.

"There is no ideology involved in local politics, nothing substantial. It's all about: we have an infrastructure project we need to get done. How can we do it most effectively and efficiently? And if you go to town board meetings, most of them are operated that way. If you look at them, you wouldn't know who is a Democrat or Republican, if you didn't know them. That's what I love about town politics and that's why it's so important that you get good people at any level, and when you get good people at the town level, it lifts everybody up."

Potholes get fixed locally, not in Washington. That's why in any party, it's most important to find the best candidates, "build the bench" and give them all the technical know-how to get them elected.

A good strategist would or should have a sense of which local races are or aren't possible to win. You can't win them all and you have to pick the ones you feel you win, and throw all your support behind those candidates.

State races have their own teams of professionals to assist, but local candidates generally rely on county parties for support. In Mr. Cardinale's case as Democratic county chair, he is the ultimate volunteer: He draws no salary, nor benefits, and he pays his own way to get into all the political events. Talk about giving back to the community!

Looking for a campaign manager, you would go through their résumés and look at campaigns they've worked on, then interview them and find out what exactly they did, whom they worked for. Did they work with people who advised on policy? Did they work with people who developed strategy? Did they work with people who did TV ads, who did video ads, who did mailers? What kinds of resources and what connections do they bring? You have to listen carefully and be skeptical of the "perfect" answers. Question them on the finer details and discuss each potential campaign manager with your team before making a hasty decision.

A seasoned campaign manager is invaluable for running a successful campaign. Friendship with your candidate should not be a factor for being one's campaign manager, running a campaign. It's warfare and if you're not prepared to go to war with a winning attitude for your candidate with both guns blazing, back off and ride your horse into the sunset. Your candidate will have a greater chance of losing because of you. Make a palatable excuse and remain friends on that level. There's too much at stake otherwise.

Richard Croce said, "Although I have spent some time as an elected official, I enjoyed the seven campaigns I have managed over the last fifteen years more. Both were challenging but rewarding.

"My elected offices were town board and county legislator. I actually ran against my former father-in-law and beat him. We didn't do any negative campaigning, and the family stayed together afterwards… until I got divorced. It was humorous in the community and an interesting twist in a rather boring town board campaign.

"My father-in-law examined the finances of the police and wanted to make some changes. Once you mobilize the police and firemen back then, everybody is going to vote against you. Then you don't have a chance. Absolutely. They all seem to support each other. Highway department, too, and town employees.

"For me, it wasn't always about adding legislation to try to fix every problem that came before the boards, and there were many! I was more concerned that the boards did not spend other people's money foolishly. Although, I have to laugh, I was the deciding vote to pass a "temporary" increase in the sales tax, twenty-three years ago this May 13th. The lesson learned is that sometimes you do have to hold your nose and vote against your principles when there are no other good options.

"My campaign management experience was three campaigns for elected judges, and another was for a district attorney for three cycles. Each campaign presents its own set of circumstances that have to be managed and worked through. Much depends on the demographics and the affiliation of the candidate. Although the candidates I supported were all in the minority, all but one won his race. In the county-wide races that I was involved in, all candidate brought their friends, relatives and neighbors to assist with the effort. Sometimes meetings were like trying to herd cats and there were plenty of opinions offered as to how to win the race! At times, meetings could get pretty heated and I would have to restore order. I would always remind the members of the committee that there would be no reward for second place. It is winner take all. "
-Richard Croce, campaign manager, the Hudson Valley area in New York

The challenge is huge and the responsibilities, endless. You, as campaign manager, are the conductor of an orchestra, directing every instrument to meld into the sound and energy of one great symphony, creating beautiful music in various movements, and reaching a harmonic crescendo of strings, woodwinds, tympani, horns, and crashing cymbals into the march toward a victorious election climax.

"**The 'Green Team,'** as strategist Diana Spada describes it, **"is the inner core of four to six people who run a local campaign.** It consists of the candidate, campaign manager, campaign strategist, treasurer, family member and close friend of the candidate's who has earned the trust of the team. This is the candidate's think tank. Other peripheral members are social media consultants who work on websites and social media sites and polling experts. It depends on the size and importance of the campaign (money available as well).

These are the people who formulate a campaign plan, strong message and platform, scheduling appearances and press releases, speechwriting, article and editorial writing, newspaper deadlines, research, both positive and negative, budget, and all other endless details, including polling, voter research provided by your board of elections, fundraising, advertising, volunteers' assignments, printing and knowing that your printing company can turn your literature out in 24-48 hours, signage, physical appearance, press relations, the paying of bills, transportation and incidentals. Organization is the key to an effective campaign.

But in larger national, state-run and district campaigns, one needs to try to have the following staff members: At the top, the chief of staff/operations, campaign manager, county coordinator, finance director/treasurer, office manager, legal advisor, scheduler, research director, speechwriter, website and media manager, advertising director, press secretary, secretary, bookkeeper, advance travel person, volunteer director, driver(s) and election day chairperson (very, very Important).

It's simply thrilling. There is absolutely nothing sweeter than your candidate's arms raised in victory to a cheering audience. All that work, all that effort, all that support, all that planning, all those collective hopes and dreams exploding in ecstatic cheers as your final slashing baton slices the frenzied air filled with raining confetti, balloons, hugs and kisses.

As Diana Spada was told by a local elected official, '"Money is the mother's milk of a campaign." An effective campaign manager has to be proficient in relating to and handling political and party people. He or she also has to have the personality to convey confidence and trust in him or herself, has to be acquainted with and be able to socialize with the power people, and, extremely importantly, have the ability to raise "Mother's Milk." Campaigns need money. No money, no message, less advertising, TV, radio, printing, staff. "Money makes the campaign world go 'round, go 'round, go 'round. Money makes the world go 'round. It makes the world go round." ("Carousel") Sorry, I don't mean to sound crass, but that's reality. How true it is.

If you are asked to become the campaign manager for a potential candidate, accept **only** if you believe in that candidate and that that candidate can win, as well as one who will buy into your campaign plans, including aggressively knocking on doors and/or standing in front of subway stations and bus stops. If you have **any** doubt about that candidate's chances, politely decline the offer. You cannot put your whole heart into an election campaign if you do not have total faith in that candidate. It would be a waste of your time and deceitful if you accepted.

You have to have confidence that your candidate is a potential winner, and not some person whose ears are plugged with cotton balls. He or she might be well-educated, a respected professional, with a perceived ability to do the job, but who will simply not listen to the party committee regarding his or her agenda. True, one has to have energy, conviction and belief in one's self, but must also be open to ways of softening the message, if necessary.

If that agenda is extremely controversial and the candidate's opinions are immovable and not popular with one's constituency, even after being told that he or she will lose the election and will not get the party's support, dump him or her. Losing an election serves no purpose.
It's Important to relate to voters by telling a story about yourself:

How to be a hero: The Powerful Narrative of a Compelling Story by Mark McKinnon, a Political Strategist of note, in a *New York Times* movie, "How To Win An Election" by Sarah Klein and Tom Mason, states that successful political campaigns tell great stories. Imagine sitting around a teacher, engrossed and hanging on every word, and that's what this short movie is all about.

"Every campaign," he says, "has to have a simple narrative for the candidate to identify" and convey in an understandable manner. The narrative has to identify a threat or opportunity, as well as a villain who threatens, and a denied opportunity effecting disgruntled, scared voters.

The scenario also stars a hero, who can come to the rescue on his or her white horse, resolve the problem, make a deal, and ride off into the sunset to the White House or state house or county government center, village hall or justice court.

"That's the classic narrative architecture for candidates" from "How to Win an Election," and it is incredibly compelling in getting people to believe in the candidate. Telling an emotional story of trials and tribulations with a happy ending is very powerful, but the story must have a human, moral conviction to get that message across to voters.

On July 26th, 2016, Hillary Clinton was nominated at the Democratic convention in Philadelphia to become the first woman Presidential candidate in American history. Whether you're a Democrat, Republican, or a member of another party, this is an extraordinary moment for all who believe in true equality and women's rights.

On that night of July 26th, her husband, former President Bill Clinton, took to the podium and delivered one of his greatest speeches, a narrative of his life with Hillary, and how it all began when they were law students at Yale. He wove that narrative in with her life as an activist from the very beginning and her desire to help those in need that continues to this very day.

He mentioned marriage and family, of her balancing her responsibilities between motherhood and a political life as a public servant. He talked of the highs and lows and her resolve and perseverance, intelligence and warmth, and determination to be of service to America as a "change maker."

As the author, I try to be totally neutral in this book, as mentioned before. Party affiliation and my personal beliefs have nothing to do with the contents in this book. President Clinton's speech technique and his method of presentation and delivery is a lesson to be learned by **any** public servant in any party or anyone, for that matter, who wishes to be an effective public speaker.

President Clinton mesmerized his audience with a nuanced speech, which sounded more like a highly, personal discussion. In musical terms it went from pianissimo to a crescendo, without all the overly loud, overly dramatic stridency from one speaker after another. Ravel's "Bolero" comes to mind. It's worth listening to. I don't know why so many speakers feel the need to yell at their audience without letup or nuance, and when they do, it reduces the effectiveness of the messages they are trying to convey. You almost want to stuff your ears with cotton or earplugs.

Microphones and speaker systems in large venues and large catering halls are generally of very high quality, and one should not feel the need to shout at people. A lower voice slowly building up to the conclusion of a speech is a far stronger voice than one level of loud shouting. Non-stop shouting is grating and doesn't help in expressing one's ideas and message.

Practice your speech so that it doesn't sound like you're reading it. Make notes as to where to look up at your audience. Look up often and pace it. If you're using a teleprompter, do not always face just left or right. Train yourself to look center directly at your audience to make them feel like they are the only people in the room.

Mr. McKinnon said that people respond to fear, and his campaigns play on peoples' emotions and all the things they worry most about. People can be seduced and influenced by stories and it is important that voters try to learn everything and question every word before making a decision, and that's what democracy is all about.

To summarize: **Campaigns must have a theme** that identifies a threat, a villain, fear, hope and, in the end, a **hero**. Mr. McKinnon, Ms. Klein and Mr. Mason deserve to be the true heroes for every prospective candidate entering the fray.

"We must dare to be great; and we must realize that greatness is the fruit of toil and sacrifice and high courage."
President Teddy Roosevelt

The campaign manager has to bring that narrative all together, and he or she needs the nuts and bolts of an organization to do so. On small campaigns, it is often the candidate and a few closest family members and friends doing all the work.

Very critical appointments, after chief of staff and campaign manager, are the county coordinators in district campaigns. They are people who are in touch with the pulse of the county and who know what the issues are and how information flows in and out of the county. Those coordinators have to figure out how the candidate can stand out and resonate among the citizenry.

Each coordinator sets the tone and itinerary, what media to invite and who else will have the honor of speaking at all those various county events. It's a huge responsibility and if the wrong person is selected, it will negatively impact the image of the campaign and thus, the candidate.

The campaign coordinator has to be one who has the ability to unite people and who is considered to be influential within a wide ranging network of local heavy hitters. If even one person is inadvertently missed, it causes a ruckus, and a person ignored is a person feeling scorned and, as a result, the candidate loses an important supporter.

There are just so many fences to mend, so ya gotta mind the store.

Congressman Chris Gibson states, "So that is a key thing in choosing a county coordinator. You can't rush to judgment. I go through elected officials; chairmen for the parties, Republican, Conservative, Independent, and then start to work out from there to the elected leaders, and maybe then faith-based advocacy groups, veterans, teachers, firefighters, policemen. At a certain point, a month or two, six weeks in, you're in a position to start to reach out and ask somebody if they want to take it on.

"We'll have a central campaign of campaign director, financial director, a team of those people, including my wife, who is probably my closest advisor. She's a social worker, knows people really well, an incredible woman, a real good listener and a real good reader of character.

"She was from a family of service and came to this experience with a whole set of diverse experiences: Social worker doing individual therapy and group therapy and a supporter of the Family Radiance Group in the military."

Congressman Gibson then explains his feeling that campaigns require a shared vision, a buy-in to one's philosophy, and the strong work ethic it takes to be smart about the way a campaign has to be built up.

A county coordinator has to make sure that appearances by a candidate throughout a district be as equal as possible within each county. Certainly, though, the more populated areas will require more attention, but counties cannot be ignored and citizens need to have the impression that their local, pressing issues are addressed.

CHAPTER 5
DO YOU REALLY NEED A CONSULTANT?

Hiring a consultant: Small, local campaigns can easily be conducted without the expertise of a consultant, but larger ones often rely on them by necessity.

Consultants do the research with voter registrations, tone of the candidacy in positive and negative campaigning, polling, mail campaigns, advertising direction, formulating the message, organizational responsibilities, demographics.

It is important to carefully interview prospective consultants, making sure they're not just blowing smoke by giving answers that are meant to please, but say nothing. Some can be regarded as "know-it-alls" and are so arrogant that they fail to listen to the candidate and the respective team.

A lot of candidates avoid hiring consultants because of the high expense with a limited budget. In one local campaign, the consultant's fee was $6,000. out of a budget of $60,000. that Richard Croce, campaign manager, worked on. That's a very significant part of one's budget in local elections, and thus the reluctance.

Frame your questions carefully and get a feel for a prospective consultant, especially when you're paying big bucks for his or her services.

Mr. Croce told me of a phone conversation incident between him, his candidate at the time and a professional consultant:

Mr. Croce was working on the campaign for a candidate with very limited funds and who then reached out to a friend in higher office. That person provided the candidate with his personal consultant, a fellow out of Albany.

It turned out that the consultant was a very aggressive fellow and who wanted the candidate to run a fairly negative campaign against his opponent, but the candidate was totally against that and refused to do so.

Mr. Croce relates, "One of the funniest things I remember about that campaign is they must've had a conversation, and I'm in my office, and my phone rings. I pick it up and it was my candidate and he was livid, and then I get an immediate other call, and asked my candidate to hold on. It was the consultant, so the consultant says something and I tell him to hold on a minute and I go back to my candidate, talk to him a minute and tell him to hold on a minute and I go back to the consultant, and I just let them vent without venting to each other. They're venting to me. Neither of them knew the other was on the other line.

"I'll never forget that the consultant said something like, 'What does the fucking hick think he's doing? He doesn't know what the fuck he's doing!' I said, 'Hold on,' and I went back on the other line to my candidate.

"We never ran the negative print stuff the consultant wanted to run. My candidate, a Republican, was running in a three-way race against two Democrats, so there was no way my candidate was ever going to lose, no way in the world. You'd never know that, though, going in."

So much for that "expert" from Albany.

Strategist **Diana Spada** interviewed a consultant for a judicial campaign who, she said, "Yessed me to death. Yessed me to death," when he answered different questions the exact same way. He was oblivious to all the research she had done: all the manuals, graphs, information about target mailings and where to walk for door-to-door campaigning and paid no attention. She prides herself on being a numbers person. He wanted $16,000.; $8000. up front and $8000. a month before the election. They hired him but she was the one running the "show." It was a very bad mix, and four years later, when the incumbent ran again, and after the campaign manager interviewed a number of consultants, she ultimately ended up with the job. In her case, unpaid. She always volunteered her services if she believed in her candidates, Party notwithstanding. She was totally independent and non-enrolled in order to freely pick and choose the candidates for whom she would work.

Ms. Spada said, "I'm a strategist and my background is law, so I'm very interested in opposition research and strategy and I like seeing why people do things, and that was the motivation for it and how we put it together to formulate the message."

The lesson is that consultants are not gods and if they're tone deaf to the desires of the candidate and the candidate's inner core team (Ms. Spada's "green team"), that person will ultimately destroy the harmony of the team. Harmony is a key component among intimates who work together day after day on behalf of candidates, and oversized egos are very destructive, especially if that consultant hasn't done his or her homework thoroughly enough to understand a candidate's opponents and platform. Campaign managers and chiefs of staff have the responsibility to maintain that harmony and ego balance.

Harvey Lippman is a former consultant and was special assistant to Governor Jerry Brown during Mr. Brown's very first term as California governor, and for the late New York congressman Allard Lowenstein. He met Governor Brown at Congressman Lowenstein's request, to help the Governor's troubled administration. For the California position, Mr. Lippman was paid a salary, as it was not a voluntary campaign position.

Congressman Lowenstein was assassinated while serving in office, and at the time, Mr. Lippman was Congressman Lowenstein's chief political advisor. Mr. Lippman stated that he only worked with people he believed in and did it out of a sense of commitment. He never accepted money for his political work as a consultant.

Mr. Lippman said that, "One of the things that amazes me now is that when you go on television, there are a group of people who make this their livelihood and it's like working for Pepsi and then the next thing, you're working for Coke, and they go from campaign to campaign.

"They are political people. They are paid political operatives. It's like how some of these people can be working for candidates whose views are so disparate that's amazing to me. My reasons for supporting a candidate are because I believe in that candidate. It's not because I want a job. It's not because I need a job as a political operative. I never took a nickel for working in political campaigns, because that was not what I was doing it for."

Campaign strategist **Diana Spada** said, "I'm not enrolled. I'm an independent voter and still very much involved in politics. I pick and choose my candidates and I love it. I support Democrats as well as Republicans. It's a matter of conscience." She has worked on assembly, district attorney and judicial races and says, "If I'm working on an issue-oriented campaign with a candidate who's willing to be honest and deal with the issues and believes in what he or she is saying, I'm in all the way.

"Politics is the necessary evil to do good. You have to go through that process to be able to effectuate chance and to do good and help people… You know, I grew up in a time when politics helped people, became so discouraged. Party politics was not for me. Party politics doesn't work for me. Everybody worries about the party, they worry about the image of the party, they worry about this, they worry about that and they don't care about the people that they're representing. They're not honest and that's part of what we're seeing right now with the presidential elections."

Candidates must have a detailed plan of action, as well as a good message and effective campaign slogan. Campaign slogans are extremely important. Make a list of possibilities created by yourself and strategists. Team members can help with slogans, as well. Pare them down and see which slogan feels right for you. What's important is that it catches on with the public and is seen on every bit of printed and Internet matter.

Strategists, ideally, must believe in their candidates and slogans are a very effective tool in the promotion of a candidate. There are tons of slogan ideas on the Internet from which you can reference. I don't know if they're copyrighted or not, so be careful and do not copy any unless you're positive they're not copyrighted, but these will be extremely helpful and it will be easy coming up with your own. Just Google "Campaign Slogans." You can mix and match and easily make a selection of your own from which to choose.

CHAPTER 6
THE ABSOLUTE IMPORTANCE OF THE BOARD OF ELECTIONS

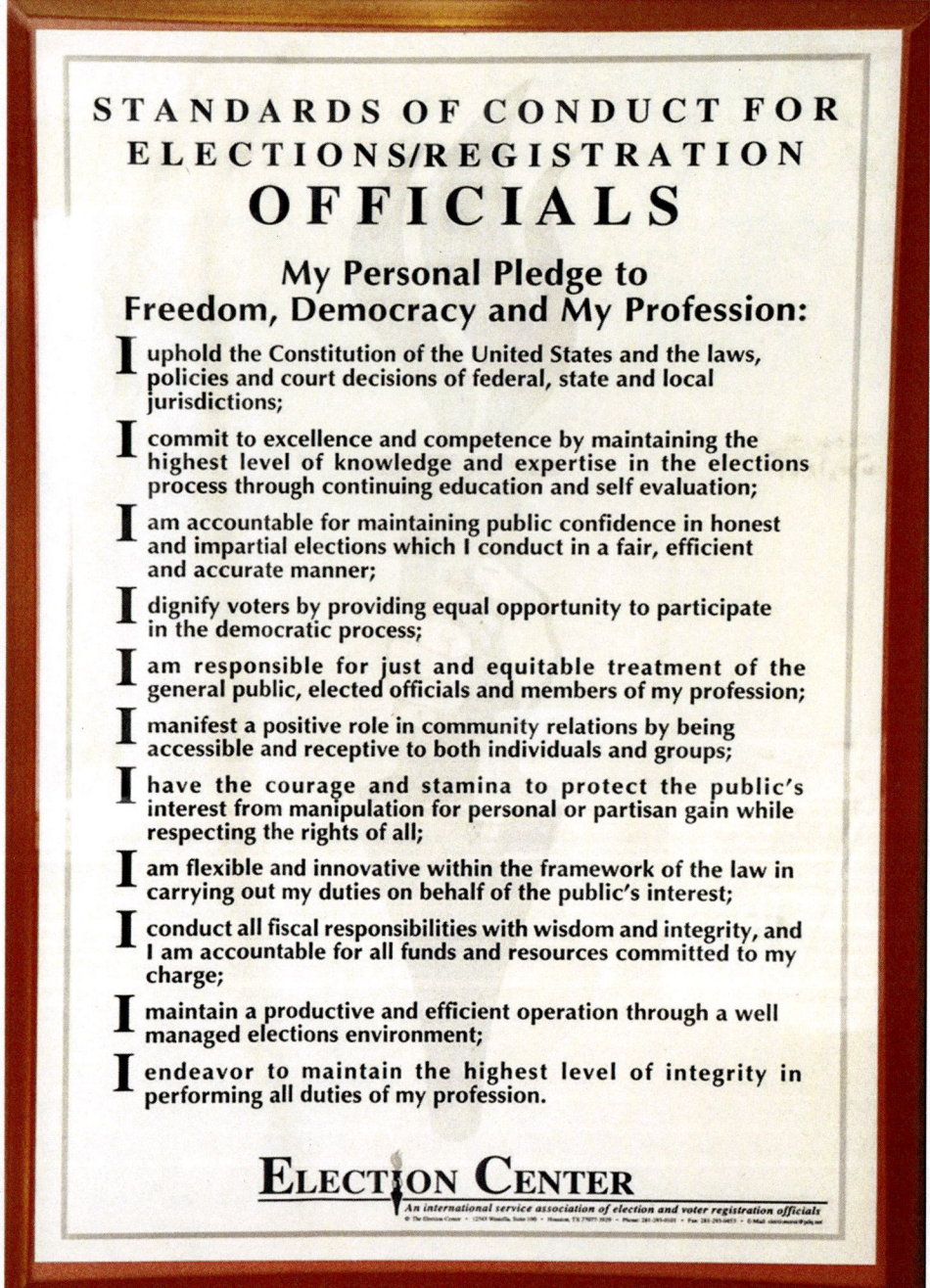

This is hanging in the reception area of the Board of Elections, Kingston, NY

Your board of elections will be critical to the difference between one's winning or losing an election. Their lists and voter analyses are the best information you will ever have. They will save you time and money. Hit their bull's eye numbers and you will dramatically increase your chance to exalt in the thrill of an election victory.

Disclaimer: I have had invaluable assistance from both the Commissioner Vic Work, and Assistant Commissioner Ashley Dittus, of the Ulster County, NY, Board of Elections and have attempted to impart basic information for candidates in New York State as examples. **Every state has different election laws and one must research those when running for office. The examples that follow are meant to show the universal seriousness of these requirements and laws.** Be aware too, that voting laws can change year by year, and you and your campaign officials should keep apprised of those changes. The role of any board of elections in America is critical to the integrity of the system and the basis of a free democracy, whereby citizens are able to freely cast their votes for legitimate candidates.

I do not claim to be an expert in this field. I'm not. The experts and electoral representatives upholding our standard of fair play of "one person, one vote," are those who serve the public in their respective Boards of Elections positions. Their service protects us all from voter fraud and we depend upon them to uphold the highest oversight level of representative American public service by ensuring that every candidate and voter gets a fair shake.

One of the great political strategists and campaign managers I've met for local elections is the Commissioner of The Board of Elections for Ulster County, NY, Mr. Vic Work. He's a passionate, intense fellow who does not mince words. He looks you in the eye and doesn't hesitate to speak his mind. He reminds me of my late Uncle Max Shabus, a World War II combat veteran, old-world tough and intensely honest, with the biggest heart, but just don't cross him. If you're of the same character, you will have someone who happily gives of himself.

Mr. Work shared his strategy with me, including his *"Winning Close Elections"* power point presentation, for which I'm most grateful to have received. If you're a new candidate and even an incumbent, his advice is invaluable and universal. It might pertain to a regional, upstate area, but his truisms and advice are lessons on any universal, strategic, election level in any state or county.

Of course, there are the most sophisticated political strategists working on very high level campaigns; presidential, senatorial, congressional, etc., with large ad agencies and polling outfits and speechwriters and all types of other aides, but Mr. Work's advice is down-home, grassroots, political strategy for candidates in communities who might never reach those exalted levels, but who nevertheless, want to make a go of it. His advice will help you jump off the diving board into the political pool. The height of the splash is up to you.

Campaign manager Richard Croce says that the board of elections voter analyses information is of the utmost importance. "Oh, yeah! You go through all that stuff. It's absolutely critical. You have to know your base. You have to know where you're gonna get your votes from and so you usually start with that and you look at the *'most likely to vote'* list and they'll give you the people who've voted. You don't know how they voted, but the most likely of the Democrats or Republicans who vote, most likely the Independents how they would vote, if you had the Independent line.

"They have it for every election. The *'most likely to vote'* are the ones who don't just vote in the Presidential campaign. We wanted a list of people who were in the primaries before."

Mr. Cardinale states, "You have to find out who voted in specific past elections and those are the people you concentrate on. You would come up with a finite number of people when you think you need to win the election and go to the base that is likely to vote for your candidate to make sure you get them out to vote. And then you work on the 'NOPs,' No Other Parties, those who are not registered to vote, and try to influence them to get out and vote for your candidate. Most times, you try to identify voters by calls: setting up a phone bank and ascertaining how you feel their responses were to the call; whether they're likely to vote for your candidate or not. If you feel they're not going to vote for the candidate, you then scratch them off the list and not bother to call back.

"You build that database, and that's the first thing you do." If you have the time, go after voters from the opposing parties. In local elections, it's all much more personal and often times, voters will vote either for candidates they know or who are known to live in their communities for numerous years.

"To say they're not popularity contests would be lying, because sometimes they are. They are."

Plan a visit to the commissioner of the board of elections: I think that more than anything else, initially, one should pay a personal visit to the commissioner of the board of elections in your city or county and introduce yourself. Do it one on one. No campaign manager, no staff member. Let him or her know who you are, and simply have a warm, private conversation. They are professionally neutral, but can be powerful allies. **Make nice.**

The New York State Board of Elections website has all the required information for candidates who are running for office. The link is "Running For Office." Every state board of elections has a website for you to use.

On the state or federal level, if you're running for governor, attorney general, or state comptroller, you have to be nominated by the state's convention and acquire 25% of the delegates in order to be on the primary ballot. If you aren't able to get 25% of the delegate votes and still want to run, you will have to get enough signatures on your petition to put you on the ballot. It's usually 5%, set by the state, but the percentages are all different and the numbers required depend on the size of the election. For state positions, the numbers of names required are much higher, of course, than senate or assembly districts.

On more local elections for county executive, county judge, district attorney and county legislature, one would need petitions.

If only one candidate has enough signatures on a petition, a primary is not necessary, for that position and that candidate will appear on the ballot in November. PETITIONS ARE NECESSARY TO GET YOU ON THE PRIMARY BALLOT IF THERE IS MORE THAN ONE ELIGIBLE CANDIDATE.

The important thing is this: **You NEED enough valid signatures on your petition to get on the ballot. You cannot get elected if you're not on the ballot.** Always get many more than required because your opposition will contest what they perceive to be the iffy ones, and those would be disqualified. The board of elections recommends that candidates get two to three times the number of signatures required just to be safe so that one would ultimately have enough of the required

valid number to **avoid duplicate signatures** (people signing for both or more candidates during the petition cycle), unqualified signers or, where you truly get petition sheets knocked off and issues with your witnesses, the witnesses being those who collect the signatures.

If you're running for countywide office in one of the designated parties (Democrat, Republican, Conservative, for example), 5% of the TOTAL ENROLLED VOTERS in your party who voted in the last three elections are required to fulfill the required number of names on your petition. But ONE WOULD NEED ONLY 1000 SIGNATURES. If you're running as an independent candidate, you will need many more countywide signatures from voters throughout the county, not the many fewer signatures than if you're a member of the designated parties.

For example, in a New York county, such as Ulster, one would need to have 1500 **valid** signatures. Keep in mind that **only** those who did not sign any Designated Petition (which is done during an earlier time frame on the calendar) cannot sign or witness any independent petitions. The Board of Elections recommends that candidates get **NOPs (non-affiliated voters)** to sign and carry those petition sheets. In reality, only town candidates typically pursue the independent petitions, and they are supervisors, highway superintendents, clerks, town board, etc.

When you have your petition ready, you need to file with the correct board of elections (the state board, county board, etc.), as prescribed by the State Board of Elections, early in the calendar year.
If you are NOT AN ENROLLED MEMBER OF THE PARTY in which you're seeking designation, you will have to file a CERTIFICATE OF ACCEPTANCE. If you're in the party, you do not have to do so.

THE PARTY CHAIR OF THE PARTY IN WHICH YOU'RE SEEKING DESIGNATION ALSO HAS TO FILE CERTIFICATE OF AUTHORIZATION.

THE CANDIDATE HAS TO FILE A CERTIFICATE OF ACCEPTANCE. These forms are available at the Board of Elections and the timeframe to file them is designated in the Political Calendar. You can pick up the forms when you file the petitions.

If your candidacy is just countywide, then you'd file with your local county's board of elections, but if your petition is for a multi-county district or state election, you would then have to file it with the New York State Board of Elections.

JUDICIAL candidates are exempt form these filings. If they do not want a party's designation, they will have to file a **CERTIFICATE OF DECLINATION.**

State Supreme Court judges are nominated at party judicial nominating conventions.
Candidates must list their **local residence address on the petition, as well as a PO Box,** if they have one. **NOBODY LIVES IN A PO BOX: You will have your petition automatically REJECTED if a signer only lists a PO Box for an address on a designated petition. The signer MUST list a PLACE of residence and a PO Box, if he or she has one. If not, that signature will be rejected, as well. That's why it says "BOTH" on the top.**

CANDIDATES MUST LIST THEIR TOWN(SHIP) ON THE FORM IN WHICH THEY LIVE. DO NOT LIST THE VILLAGE OR HAMLET. EVEN IF YOUR MAILING ADDRESS IS IN A DIFFERENT COMMUNITY, YOU MUST LIST THE TOWN(SHIP). That goes for ANY township in any county in the state. As an example, your property tax bill shows your township. If in doubt, either Google a county map for your Township within your county or go to your local board of elections, and they will help you find your Township of residence with their map.

THIS IS CRITICAL INFORMATION FOR YOU: YOUR DESIGNATED PETITION APPLICATION FORM CAN BE CHALLENGED WITHOUT THAT CORRECT TOWNSHIP INFORMATION.

THE GOOD LORD SAYS, "KNOW THY TOWNSHIP."

You will need someone, a professional, if possible, who knows what he or she is doing, to save your political rear end if you feel you cannot do it yourself.

Here is a PowerPoint presentation for campaign managers and political strategists by Vic Work:

This is excerpted and edited with Mr. Work's permission.

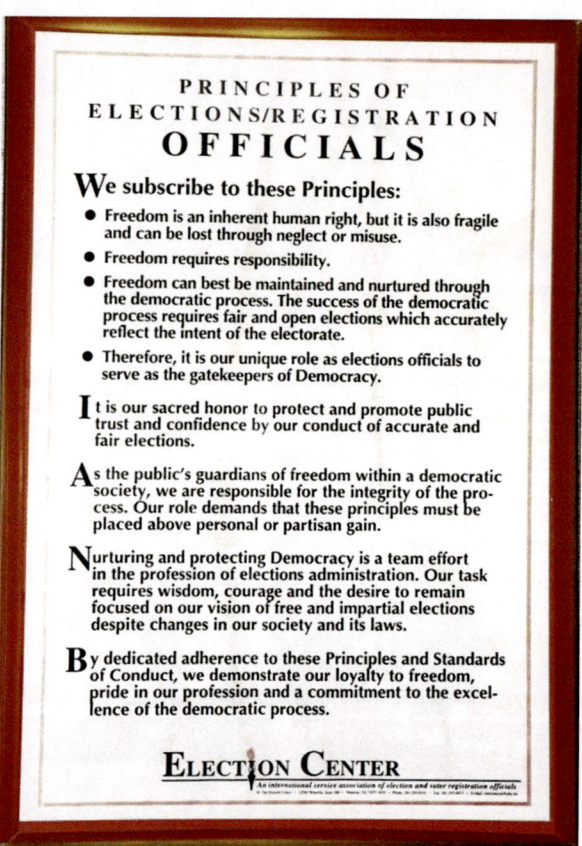

This is hanging in the reception area of the Board of Elections, Kingston, NY

"It's No Fun To LOSE, So Don't LOSE:"
-Vic Work, commissioner, Board of Elections, Ulster County, NY

★ **Get a good candidate, one you can support.**
★ **Start by contacting your board of elections!**

★ DO YOUR HOMEWORK:
- What Town, Village, County, Assembly District, State Senate, Congressional District is your candidate running in?
- Where does the candidate live? What district? What are the demographics of the area? Who lives there, where do they go to school, to shop, to play?
- What political committees are there and how active? How organized? Has the candidate run before for some office?
- Who are the local contacts for the Political Party: Democratic, Republican, Conservative, Independence, Green, Working Families, etc.?
- Does the candidate have a well-known name, large extended family, lots of friends and associates and good personal presentation?

★ WORK UP A REVERSE CALENDAR:
- It helps keep the campaign focused.
- Insures that you order things on time.
- Gives you time to add items as you go along- phone banks, doing mailings, events your candidate should attend, Helps with your campaign budget and fundraising targets.

★ MEDIA AND ADVERTISING:
- Make a website and Facebook page, LinkedIn page and other social media accounts.
- Do a survey of local media, get cost estimates, area coverage by each media- i.e. numbers of daily and weekly papers, multiple cable outlets, billboards, cable access TV channels, numbers of radio stations.
- Start working on a platform and simple media message.
- Don't ignore free media- letters to the editor, local cable TV, press releases.

★ MESSAGES:
- What is happening locally?
- What solutions does your candidate offer?
- What qualifications?
- Start by writing all the County Committee members in the District with an introduction letter from the candidate.
- Include some teasers about why the candidate is running.

-Make a list of everyone you know in your community: relatives, friends, business contacts, as they are the first targets for a fundraising letter.

-If you are not going to be self-funded, then you need to set up events, or better, get people to set them up for you with little or minimum cost. You do not want to be in the position of laying out $3000.00 or raise $3000.00.

★ HOW DO YOU GET ON THE BALLOT?
-Petitions:
-How many signatures do you need for each endorsement?
-Who will carry the petitions? Who will keep track of how many signatures and filing dates?
-When you file them, then what do you do?

★ PETITIONS:
-Higher Office than Town or Village or Town or Village Offices on a Non-Constituted Party- WFP, IND, or Green Party
-If you are not an enrolled member of the party you will need to file a Certificate of Acceptance and the Party Chair will have to file a Certificate of Authorization, unless you are running for a Judicial Office.

★ CAUCUS (USUALLY FOR TOWN RACES):
-Need to know when the local caucuses are being held for each party and where.
-Talk to the town chairs or county chairs if no town chairs.
-Look at the lists of registered members of your party or the party from which you are attempting to be nominated.
-Call everyone you know on that list and ask them to come to the caucus.
-Normally in the caucus you will have someone nominate you and someone to second your nomination.
-You are usually then allowed to speak.
-Be sure you get your supporters to the caucus so the result is not a surprise.
-If you lose the caucus vote you are done, if that is the way the office is nominated.
-If you are not a member of the party doing the caucus, you will have to sign a Certificate of Acceptance and the Caucus chair and Secretary both have to sign the Nomination Form, which is a Certificate of Nomination.
-Without the Certificate of Acceptance, you will not be on the Line for that office. Non-Constituted Parties have to do nominations by Petition (WFP, Independence, Green, etc.)

★ CAMPAIGN LITERATURE:
-Create a brochure. In brief, it should explain who your candidate is.
-It can be a tri-fold, with Candidate's photo (professional headshot) on the front, a family photo on the back fold, contact information, email, website, Facebook page, phone numbers, etc., for the middle fold.
-Inside the brochure, you should have <u>THREE KEY WORDS</u>
describing the candidate, such as: FATHER, BUSINESSMAN, ASSEMBLYMAN. Then describe each of the three words with pertinent information.

-Have it ready for the petition carriers to carry during the time they are getting signatures, and be ready to mail a PERSONAL LETTER along with the brochure to each person who signed the petitions, and most importantly, to each person who carried them.

-Have bumper stickers printed and include those with each letter, and ask each person to volunteer for your campaign.

-Be ready, if there is a primary, to mail this brochure to each party member who had voted in the past 4 (FOUR) elections or primaries. Ask them to get out and vote for you in the primary.

★If there is no primary, then mail that piece to the same group in early October.

★ ATTEND EVENTS:

-Make sure you note all the 4th of July parades and the county Firemen's parade, and be ready with signs and/or a FLOAT for Parades.

-There could be a thousand or more volunteer firemen and thousands of people watching, and you need a float in that parade or a big sign carried in front of you with people passing out helium balloons with your name on them.

-You need to be at the county fair, along with volunteers, brochures, signs and posters. This is to register voters and test out your Campaign Persona!!!! There are tens of thousands of people attending a county fair.

-The party will have a booth and you should share the cost of it and take full advantage with signs and brochures. This is an ideal place to practice your voter spiel- no one will remember other than shaking hands with the candidate.

-In the first week of August, be prepared to start Voter ID phone calls to the Not-Enrolled in Any Party Voters, followed by Direct Mail.

-If you are in a primary- Start the Voter ID for your party members as soon as you can.

-A Simple Call Script (besides a nice greeting): "Do you know there is a primary and do you plan to vote?"

- "What are the most important issues (for the office you are running for) that affect you?"

- "If the election were held today, whom would you vote for? Recite a list of the candidates."

★ SCORE THE RESULTS AS THE FOLLOWING

- "1" supporting you, "3" undecided and "5" voting for the other candidate.

-Send the "3" a piece of literature, your brochure or palm card, that might convince them to support you. Send the "1" a bumper sticker and a volunteer form.

-Make sure you do NOT call the "5s" or remind them in any way about the election!

★ AFTER THE PRIMARY:

-Your party Committee probably runs a well-coordinated campaign, trying to bring everyone together to work together for the benefit of all the candidates. This allows for sharing of information and coordination of literature drops, door-to-door and, most importantly, the GOTV effort (GET OUT THE VOTE). -IT DEPENDS ON VOLUNTEERS!

★ NOW FOR THE HARD PART:

-You will need people outside your party to support you unless you are running in a party town or county with 70% registered in your party.

-Phone the NOPs (Not Registered in any Party, but who vote) and ID them if you have time. If not, call them and ask them to vote for you (34% of the registered voters).

-*GOTV (Get Out the Vote) to your party and the NOPs (Not Registered to Vote) and remind them about the upcoming election.*

*Compiled by Vic Work, commissioner, Ulster County Board of Elections, Kingston, NY.
and gratefully reproduced with his kind permission.*

CHAPTER 7
IT'S WHO YA KNOW

Creating an Organization: Wealthy candidates or incumbents who decide to run for office, like a Michael Bloomberg, would already have a huge, talented staff of political analysts and writers from his news organization. He opens the ballgame with a triple. Other candidates from famous families: the Kennedys, Bushs, Roosevelts and so on, were so well-connected with their parties that they were already sliding into second or third.

But they still had to cross home plate, just like every other candidate. Campaigns teach you, though, to not be overconfident. Be scared and do not take anything for granted. Campaigns require unremitting focus.

Petitions: Less connected candidates have to pitch better, hit harder, run the bases faster and slide home, avoiding the tag to win the game. They have to be more hands-on and know exactly what their responsibilities must be, including getting volunteers to help acquire the required signatures on petitions for getting them on the ballot. You won't even get to first base without those signatures.

You will also need endorsements and testimonials and you have to personally meet with all the key party chairs in townships and counties whose endorsements you're trying to acquire. You also must meet with newspaper editors and political staff, well-known citizens, celebrities, advocacy groups, diverse ethnic groups, labor unions (ex: teachers, police, firemen, environmentalists, women's groups, highway department, other public employees, TV and radio reporters, friends you trust, etc. Make a list of possible questions of important issues that you can be sure will be thrown at you and be prepared with informed answers. Play act and practice your responses with members of your team.

Your own party's endorsement is crucial for your campaign and additional multiple party endorsements are very important in any elections, but majorly so in local, small elections. It's sometimes difficult to win with just one party endorsement, but if you can get the endorsements of other parties besides your own, such as Conservatives or Independents, all the better for your own chances of victory. Congressman Chris Gibson said, "We won a couple of endorsements, so there was a feeling that we were going to win. These were by town committee and it was in March, and that's what March was, the endorsement process."

County Legislator **Kathy LaBuda** unequivocally says that, "In local elections, you cannot run only on one line. People from the opposing party will simply not cross over in local elections. I'm sorry, but they won't, they won't. You have to get another party's endorsement and get on another line on the ballot. I told this to two other candidates years ago and also told them to go online to the Working Party's application. The deadline was tonight. They asked are you sure and I said, 'I'm telling you, you have to get on the line!'

"One got it! The other candidate didn't listen to me because he felt he couldn't agree on every platform question. I told him not to answer those, but he never did finish that application. The fellow who did follow through won his election. You cannot win a county-wide election if you don't have the extra party lines. The guy who didn't, lost by a substantial number of votes. You gotta get that extra line **or lines** in local politics!"

Building relationships is invaluable, and particularly so for an incumbent, if one wants to be an effective public servant. If you're able to help others, your deeds will come back to you ten-fold. As Elliott Auerbach said, "It is not just public service, but rather, the 'people business,' because the people who are in your life today, whether they're coming to you looking for help, may be the people you'll turn to tomorrow to help you. So that's a great aspect of building relationships and future relationships, or even being able to bring different parties together, so that you're acting as a person in the middle who knows people on both sides of an equation and are able to coalesce and bring them together." That happens when relationships are nurtured and personal trust established. It's the art of compromise.

Adele Reiter, the Ulster County deputy county executive, stresses the importance of personal endorsements. "**Endorsements are important because** the people giving the endorsements are those who believe in you. They have your back. Every single endorsement helps you with the privilege of holding public office and those are from the people who put their trust in you. **Those endorsements are much more than just a political piece.** They are a great reminder of the promises you made to get them and why it is so important to you to keep those promises.

"**Their endorsements come with advice and expectation**, and at the end of the day, with whatever advice you may take, the decisions are ultimately your very own. But one should be a good listener when the people you trust give you their best advice that can sometimes be brutally honest. Be big enough to realize that they've given it for all the right reasons. That advice, one hopes, will make you a much more effective and responsive public servant."

You cannot sell your soul in doing so and should not just try to get extra party lines on the ballot. If you're going after extra party endorsements, understand that there may be tradeoffs and a *quid pro quo* in their endorsements. Their platforms are going to be different than yours and if you take their endorsements, think of what will they will expect in return, down the legislative line. Work those differences out first so there are no misunderstandings later.

Congressman Chris Gibson: "The national party didn't think I would win so I didn't get their support till late September. They patted my head and said, 'You look like a nice guy' and everything like that, but there really was no financial support for our campaign. We had to go out and hustle and so, it was entirely grassroots.

"**I did house parties** from anywhere from six people to sixty, maybe more. So I spent time getting to know people, and this is the part of politics I really like, listening and getting a chance to really meet people and figuring out how best I can serve them. I got a lot of support that way. I had a lot of people who learned about my background and thought about having a veteran serving us in Congress. There is an upside to that."

In smaller districts or community elections, those endorsements can mean the difference of 16, 17, 19 votes for you when people vote their party line, and that might mean the difference between heaven and hell.

Chris Petsas, Chairman of the Poughkeepsie, NY, Common council, says that "those extra lines mean extra votes. What I see is that people, candidates, are going after the ballot lines, rather than their belief in extra party platforms."

If you're your own person, though, it might simply mean the usual give and take of mutual benefit in political maneuvering. And, let's face it, those extra votes will put you over the top and in a power position in government. And **THAT** gives you the opportunity of making a real difference for your constituency.

The late Speaker of The House Congressman Tip O'Neill, reminded people that "All politics is local." That quote should be in every campaign headquarters.

You have to attend ethnic places of worship and have people of every ethnicity working for you on staff or as volunteers. If in an area with a large black population, then have black advisors with contacts in black churches, if in Hispanic or Asian or other ethnic communities, try to attract advisors from those ethnic groups. It's important to attend services in their places of worship to show your support, and try to befriend VIP's and presidents of their societies in those communities. Try, too, to get invited to their annual dinners, such as, for example, an Asian society dinner or gala, where you might be invited to make a speech.

They will appreciate your attention and feel that they will have entrée into the office for which you're running. Senior centers, retirement communities and nursing homes are readymade for your attendance. Visit as many as you can. They love the attention and they **vote** and they'll remember you and all the things you've done for them or shall be expected to do, if elected. Seniors are a huge block of votes.

Judge Anthony McGinty said, "I've campaigned with two, three or four other people, and particularly, if somebody is local, it just increases the possibility of one of you already having a personal connection with the person whose home you're visiting, and so that person takes the lead and says, "Joe, nice to see you! Haven't seen you since the VFW dinner.

Here're my friends who are running for this office and this other office. Say hello, etc." Then you can convey we're all together, we have similar values and we're all from the same party. He's running for this position. I'm running for that position. We're happy to see you today. That I think is good. It conveys a message of solidarity that we have candidates for all kinds of offices, we get along with each other, we're gonna cooperate with each other, we're out here walking together and saying hello to people. I like that."

Churches, synagogues and mosques cannot formally endorse candidates, but you should try to get speaking engagements from the pulpit in front of their congregations.

Okay, really though, so they can't formally endorse, but in their own way they will point out a candidate's platform as related to their religious beliefs.

That's human nature. You'll be expected to comment on abortion, women's rights, gay rights and marriage, immigration, belief in God and where religion fits into your platform. Practice those potential answers to avoid the pitfalls, but stick to your beliefs. Although people may vigorously disagree with you, they will respect your direct honesty and fearlessness while on their turf. JFK is a prime example in defending his religious beliefs, while separating church and state from his quest for the Presidency.

"I believe in an America that is officially neither Catholic, Protestant nor Jewish– where no public official either requests or accepts instructions on public policy from the Pope, the National Council of Churches or any other ecclesiastical source– where no religious body seeks to impose its will directly or indirectly upon the general populace or the public acts of its officials– and where religious liberty is so indivisible that an act against one church is treated as an act against all."
-President John F. Kennedy

CHAPTER 8
FINANCE COMMITTEE: MONEY MAKES THE WORLD GO 'ROUND, BUT NOT ALWAYS

Create a campaign finance committee: Considering the necessity of raising money to finance one's campaign, **you have to have a campaign finance chairman and treasurer.** You will also need a very skilled fundraiser who's had experience in raising money for other political candidates. He or she has to know the kinds of events one should be having, be it coffee klatches, meet the candidate cocktail parties, senior centers, bars or restaurants, private homes. Everyone is expected to contribute. It's a given. The account must be legally constructed and registered with the board of elections. **There are very strict rules for FILING ON TIME**, and if not, the candidate can be fined severely. Please refer to Chapter 6 for board of elections rules.

A skillful campaign manager needs to have a treasurer and must open a specific campaign account to handle all the contributions that are sent in. In small campaigns the candidates themselves will handle those finances, when necessary, if they do not have the means to hire a treasurer. Other than a campaign manager, though, a treasurer or someone handling contributions is most important, as those financial laws and required reports are most stringent.

It makes a candidate look terrible if financial reports aren't filed on time. Opponents can run with that and make it a campaign issue, accusing the opposing candidate as being so incompetent that he or she cannot even run a campaign both properly, efficiently and legally, much less running one's office. It's a potential big vote loser.

"Access Capital"
If big money is involved, what are the payoffs expected from those generous contributors? Will you be strong enough to resist their expectations of you? In response to a question of how much influence money begets, the answer from one of the seasoned political experts was that money generally brought easier access to the elected incumbent, to listen to the contributors' or lobbyists' concerns and agenda. It did not mean that the incumbent was obligated to make decisions on behalf of those contributors, but that money does seem to ensure a ready audience from the candidate or incumbent. It is simply called **"Access Capital,"** as Michael Lewis of The Carlyle Group perfectly stated in the *New Yorker* magazine article.

Some candidates will only accept contributions from small contributors in order to not be influenced unequally. You have to evaluate where you stand on this highly sensitive money issue when deciding to run.
Senator Bernie Sanders of Vermont, for instance, was one of them, making famous the average $27.00 campaign contributions he received when running for President.

It is also okay to accept in-kind contributions, but they must be reported as well, just like any other money contributions.

Candidates and their spouses may spend any amount of their OWN MONEY for their campaign, but that must be reported. One must report money transfers, housekeeping and independent expenditures.

It is not necessary to report volunteer services, unless reimbursed, travel expenses under $500.00 and house parties under $500.00, but house parties MUST be held in a HOUSE, NOT elsewhere in restaurants or catering halls. Contributions from raffles are not allowed.

If you are having a fundraising silent auction, the in-kind value of an item or product is only determined, in the end, by the amount one has paid for it, and **that** is the value of the contribution. It cannot be the suggested asking price.

Mr. Petsas, in all his campaigns, says has never accepted a dime either. "I used my own money from my own pocket. Didn't have a fundraiser. I just shelled out. If you can do it that way, it's great. I recognize that some people can't and I recognize fundraisers have different aspects of raising funds.

"'cause you know what happens? This one raises $500. and then a $1,000. from another donor, and the next thing you know is that one of the donors might have a parking meter in front of their business they want moved, a sidewalk that has a little crack in it and the sidewalk down the street has a bigger crack, but they want theirs fixed first just because they donated. I don't have any time for that. Everybody who calls me on my cellphone gets the same treatment. There's no financial connection with me and I'm not going to have one."

End the guessing game: Other candidates in smaller communities and districts, by necessity, have to run low-budget campaigns and raise money among family and friends if they don't have their own. One candidate, Dan Torres, town councilman in New Paltz, NY held a fundraiser at a local cupcake bakery and raised $1000.00. That was a considerable amount of money for him and his fundraiser was considered to be a great success.

He worked out his expenditures and knew where and how he was going to spend this money, much of it on printing and postage expenses for palm cards and mailers. To save on expenses, he had a list of prime voters provided by the board of Elections and broke it down from a very large pool of many thousands down to a few hundred.

Instead of thinking he had to print as many as 3000 palm cards and mailers, he analyzed the data and realized that he only had to print perhaps 500 of each, **going to those targeted prime voters** who voted in the last three gubernatorial elections. He ended up paying 1/5 of the cost of those printing expenses, rather than a much larger random amount that wasn't based on statistical research.

These same prime voters would also receive phone calls from the candidate at specific dates, according to the candidate's reverse calendar up to Election Day.

It doesn't matter if candidates are running in the smallest local, rural elections or the largest populous areas. **If you want to win, you have to analyze the voting data from the board of elections and give yourself the biggest edge and chance of winning.** It is also a huge money saver. Yes, Mr. Torres won, because he used his extremely limited campaign contributions wisely. His was a very smart grassroots campaign.

Attorney Harvey Lippman worked as a financial advisor for the late Congressman Allard Lowenstein, and for the current Governor of California, Jerry Brown, when Governor Brown first served as Governor in the 1970s and 80s. "My reasons for supporting a candidate are because I believe in the candidate. It's not because I want a job. It's not because I need a job as a political operative. I never took a nickel for ever working in political campaigns, because that was not what I was doing it for.

"But one of the things that amazes me now is that when you go on television, there are a group of people who make this their livelihood and it's like working for Pepsi, and then the next thing, you're working for Coke, and they go from campaign to campaign.

"They are political people. They are paid political operatives. It always amazes me. It's like how some of these people can be working for candidates whose views are so disparate; that is amazing to me."

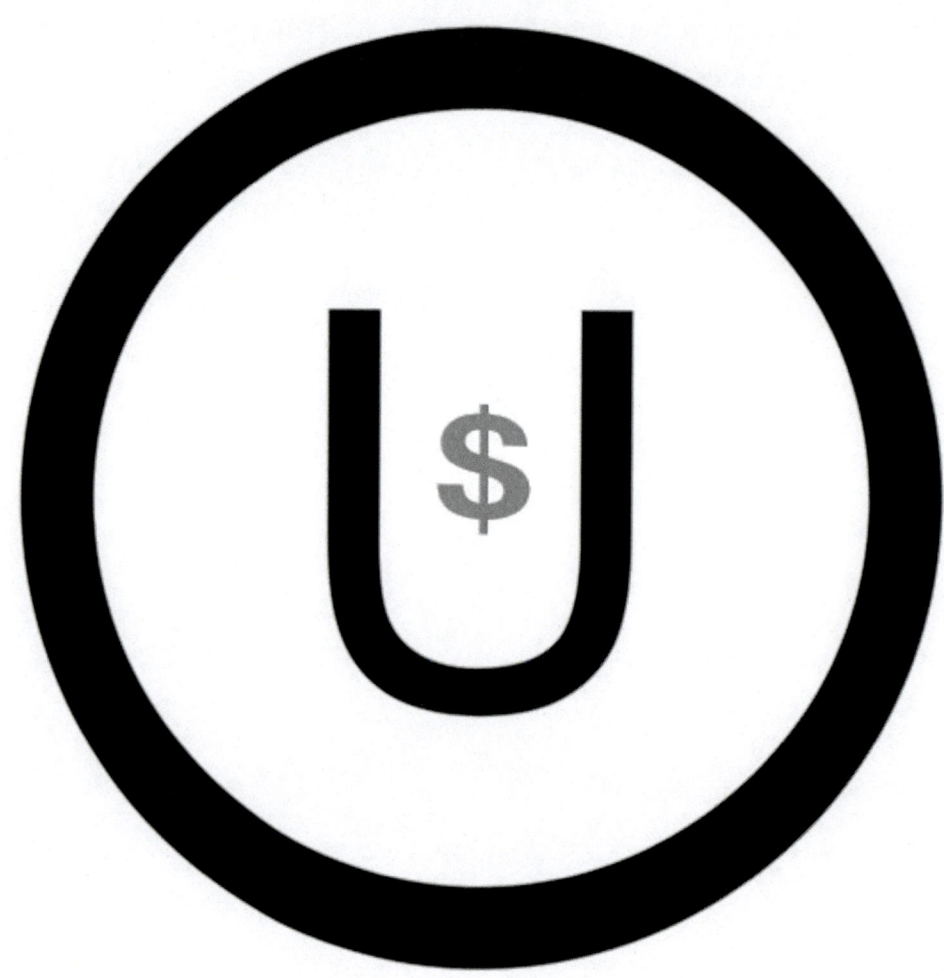

You have to make sure your $$$ contributions & finances are Kosher.

The website for the New York State Board of Elections is www.elections.ny.gov. providing you with all the information you need. Other states have their own websites. Your local board will also provide you with that information, but the state's staff makes the final determination on questionable contributions.

Handle the money with $queaky clean hands: Your contributions have to be within the legal limit for the particular office for which you're running. There are critically important charts and manuals available from that board of elections informing candidates for each office as to what the limits are, as well as critical deadlines for filing reports. You don't want any smell to hover over you if you're not paying attention. It really gets voters nauseous when the lid is opened and opponents will jump all over you with their negative campaigning. Elections can be lost by financial carelessness or recklessness. A campaign treasurer's position cannot be chosen lightly.

As Campaign Treasurer **Burt Gulnick**, states, "All of these reportings, one thing you learn as treasurer, there are reporting cycles to the Board of Elections, and there's a tool of that the board of elections gives you. **"There are different limits,** depending if it's a corporation, partnership, married couple or just a single person. Also, it depends on what office one runs for and whether one is a candidate for state office or local office."

From the New York State Board of Elections:
Contributors should be aware that political contributions are **NOT** tax deductible. Also, campaigns are NOT cash businesses. One may give in New York State no more than $100.00 in cash and the rest by check. Cash contributions must be reported.

If you only raise under $1,000., you just have to register with your local board of elections. If you've raised more than $1,000., you must register with the local **AND** state Boards of Elections.

Ulster County Comptroller **Elliott Auerbach** says, "I am very lucky that I have not had to manage my own finances or anybody else's finances. I joke with people, my treasurer is a retired Episcopal minister. Whom better to trust with your campaign funds than a minister.

"...and money, unfortunately, plays a dramatic role in politics. There's a lot of bookkeeping work that goes along with local campaigns. You have to file on time, you have to document everything."

In New York State, campaign treasurers must record every dollar that is contributed to a campaign, and continue to record after the campaign for the length of that particular office. One should set up a spreadsheet for this purpose.

If a cash contribution is received that is over $100., it must be returned. A thank you note and explanation should accompany the money. "Thank you for supporting So and So's campaign, but unfortunately, due to the State law, you have exceeded the legal limit. Enclosed is your contribution. We welcome your contribution and the limit in your category is $$$$$$$. Very sorry for the inconvenience. We are most grateful for your support. Signed."

Checks are a different animal, and again, one needs to know the money limitations if you're receiving contributions from corporations, partnerships, married couples and individuals. Also, those contributions must not exceed the cumulative limit of your term of office.

If your term is for two years, as an example, and the contribution limit is $5000.00 from a corporation, that limit cannot be exceeded during the term of office. You can't get more than that. Period. If your contribution is under $100.00 cash, you cannot receive more cash during that term of office during that election cycle.

As a treasurer, you have to report to The Board of Elections five times every year: January, July, a Primary report, thirty days prior to the election and ten days after Election Day. That information is open to the public and one can go online on the Board of Elections' website to see who contributed to whom. It can be really juicy information to see who's shelling out and for how much. You're not allowed to keep any secrets.

Some contributors will send checks that are over the limit and those must be returned. If any of that money is received with just a name and without a return address, the treasurer must make every effort to find out who that contributor was. If the treasurer cannot, that check is put aside, but that contribution must still be reported. A diligent treasurer should record and report **everything**, including the fact that he or she couldn't locate the contributor.

The state has a "non-didn't hit the limit" revenue category and the treasurer has to make a "try as you may" effort, and sometimes does not succeed in locating the contributor, so you may just put that $100.00 in a non-distributed contribution as an un-itemized donation.

So if your term is for four years, you will have the same contributing financial limits for the duration of your term.

Mr. Gulnick states, "One thing I do is document everything: any checks you receive in the campaign, for the campaign, I make copies. Any bills that you pay, I make copies. The bank has copies of the checks you wrote, but it's always good to keep them on file and one thing, the State does have up to seven years to do an audit like anything. Also, so it's always good to keep them on file. I save emails, as well, if they're important to the campaign."

About that "Housekeeping Money:" Housekeeping money for bills is paid by committee, not by individual candidates. Hmmmmmmm, this is campaign dough that is used for just about anything to pay bills: staff, entertainment, dinners, alcohol, a pool cover in one instance as told to me, rent for offices, vehicles, gas, travel, printing, postage, and even contributions to not-for-profit organizations. According to Burt Gulnick, campaign treasurer, there is a lot of leniency here. One can also use a credit card for payments.

As far as Mr. Gulnick is concerned, it is a very lenient practice and opens up a potential can of worms. It is something he is completely against and feels if abused, it is on the cusp, of illegality. It is also necessary to record every "Household Expense" and, if necessary, justify each one if audited.

New York State is very aggressive about auditing treasurers' reports, and has recently substantially expanded its staff of auditors. As I've mentioned, all states have different rules and regulations, but the key is that always each Board of Elections enforce those rules.

Mr. Gulnick stated, "The county exec. looked me straight in the eye and said, 'You're the only one I trust with the money,' when I was asked to be his campaign treasurer, and I earned that respect. That's why, in my position, I'm meticulous, and you have to be. In serving the public, that's who I work for. When people ask me, yes, I work for the county executive, but he also works for the people of Ulster County."

Check your hands and make sure they haven't gotten dirty from handling the wrong kind of contributions. You cannot simply wash your hands and walk away from that. Those are permanent stains that don't come off. If you accept contributions from shady individuals or groups with terrible reputations contrary to your beliefs, or contributions over the legal limit, you got problems!!! You're going to have to return the money if you don't want your reputation soiled. And if word gets out that your campaign accepted dirty money, even returning it doesn't make up for the remaining dirt left under your fingernails. Do you not think your opponent won't pounce on that? It's like having bad B.O. and people will be repelled if they get too close.

"No matter how many campaigns you have worked on – It's a whole new ballgame when you decide to run yourself. Be careful who you take endorsements from- if he's a congressman up on charges- you don't want it. Be careful who gives you money, too. If your money is coming from the "fat cats" who pose as a environmentalists, people are going to know you are already 'bought'".
– Marcy Goulart, former President, Ulster County, NY, Democratic Women

"The biggest part I was nervous about was how to raise money, but this time I had to ask for money and I've never asked people for anything. My party told me I had to ask for money and support my campaign. They had to be invested in my campaign and help me to get elected. I made fundraisers, which I hated. After a time, I said screw the fundraisers, it's just a bullshit way of doing what everybody else was doing, and I got on the phone and I said, "Hi," and called my friends. And they asked how much? And people started writing checks for all amounts."
– Jeff Siegel, candidate for County Legislature, Sullivan County, NY

When **Anthony T. Kane**, a Monticello, NY attorney, ran for Family Court Judge the first time, he said, "It's a lot more fun when you don't have anything to lose because my attitude was that if this didn't work out, well, I met a lot of people in the County and it just would've been good for my practice, as so it was going to be a win-win situation no matter what happened. We didn't spend much money. If the election cost $5,000. overall, it was a lot.

"So I became family court judge. When you run the second time, you've now grown accustomed to the position and grown accustomed to being a judge and don't have a law practice to go back to.

"There're now stakes involved, so it becomes a more serious undertaking. I think we spent $10,000. on that race for County Court. I raised a little more money than in the Family Court race.

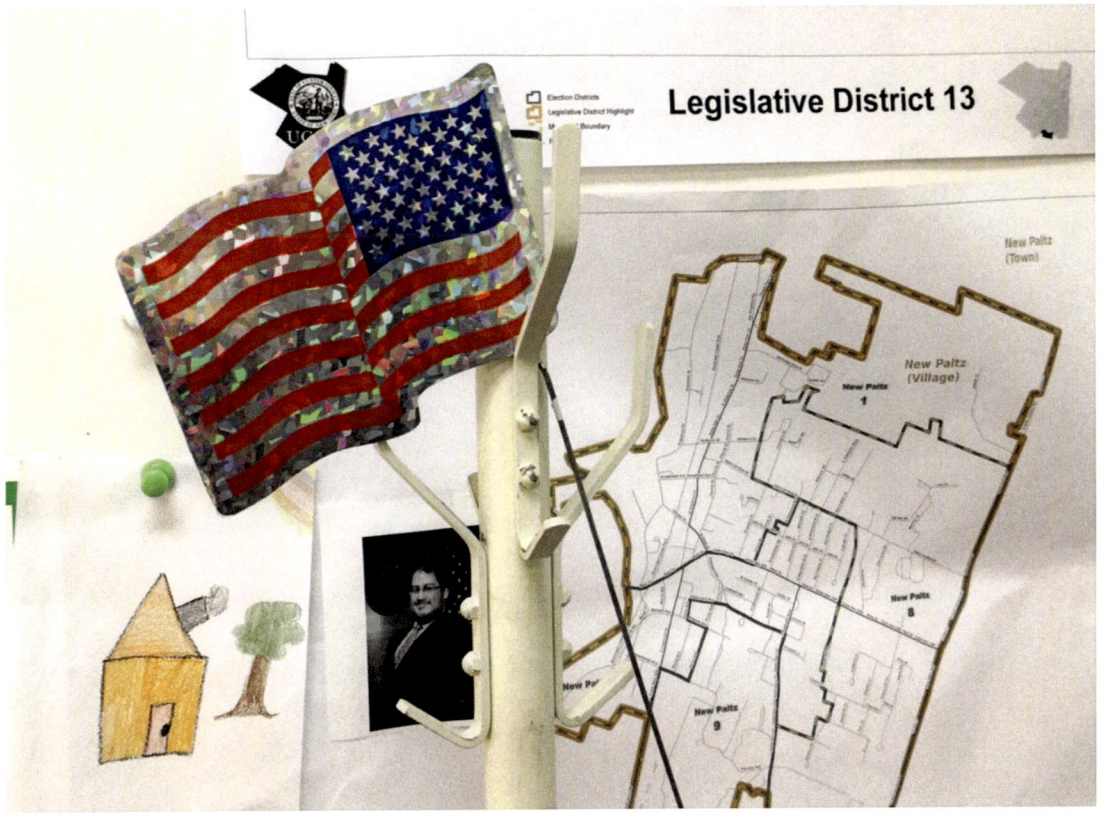

CHAPTER 9
CREATING AN ORGANIZATION

Creating an organization for a candidate is about getting all the right people together and forming a committee.

You will build a staff and involve as many volunteers as you can attract, as well as a cohesive and well thought-out game plan. Being a "gatekeeper" and limiting those volunteers who want to enter the inner sanctum to help with the campaign will work to your detriment.

IT IS NECESSARY THAT YOU, as chief of staff or campaign manager, convey a strong message to voters what the long-range goals are for your candidate who's running for lower or higher office never be over-confident.

Researching the two or three most important issues: In New York, one strategist researched issues primarily by reading articles in The New York Times and keeping up with them as they evolved. If you're running for county executive or borough president or district attorney, you have to be tuned in to all the local papers, as well. Local papers in smaller communities all discuss important, current issues. That is where candidates and incumbents must do their homework to be ready for debates or editorial board meetings and town hall meetings. Speeches, too.

For your platform, it's important for your trusted think tank to come up with two or three of the most important campaign issues. Take a poll of what concerns people most in their communities. Call people or meet them on the street and ask them what their most pressing issues are. Email and go on Facebook, as well, to ask your friends and have them ask their friends (locally).

Your research is critically important. Feedback is important. Listen closely. Rate the issues in order of importance by numbers 1 to 5. Don't get sidetracked by lesser important issues. Keep it simple so constituents are not diverted and confused. The simpler, the better. Less is **more**. Your goal is to get people to support you. Don't make the huge mistake of thinking your personal issues are **the** most important ones to consider. They're **not**.
You have to pay attention to the concerns of the public and party committee and then **pare those issues down, generally to the most important two or three, but sometimes a few more if other pressing issues are necessary.**

If you want to be silly and arrogant, don't listen, be "smarter" than anybody else, and then increase your chances for losing. I'd say that's pretty smart, wouldn't you? You have to listen.

If you're not a seasoned candidate, it would be most prudent to first run for lower office, just to get your feet wet. Learn the political process, interact with other public servants, and see how things really get done. Mr. Trump is another story, of course. The advice given by Richard Mathews is, ***"Be prepared when something comes and don't be afraid to take it."***

"A prince "...should conduct himself in such a way that greatness, boldness, gravity, and strength will be observed in his actions. In dealings with individual subjects, his decisions must be irrevocable; and he must maintain himself in such high regard that no one will ever think of cheating him or misleading him. A prince who gives this sort of account of himself will be highly esteemed; and against someone who is highly esteemed, conspiracy is unlikely."
– Niccolo Machiavelli, *The Prince*

One of **Sally Cross's** jobs was campaign pollster and voter I.D. specialist for an Oregon gubernatorial campaign of Ted Kulongowski, Congresswoman Elizabeth Furse's campaign and William Woodward III's. Her job was to make sure, among everything else, that she checked on how many calls her candidates personally made to raise money, how many doors they personally knocked on and how much of the districts they personally walked through. She cracked the whip.

For Congresswoman Furse, she took a leave of absence from her job and worked without pay for eight weeks, organizing voter identifications and the GOTV (Get Out The Vote) campaign.

Here's the key to the kingdom: This is the classic election strategy used by Ms. Cross for Congresswoman Furse's Campaign: They focused on Democrats, for example, who had a history of regular voting. They also researched the swing voters, also known as "persuadable voters," and then called all the Democrats and swing voters, asking them if they planned to vote in the upcoming election and for Ms. Furse. They could've been from any party.

They had a little script, and volunteers called each night and on weekends to constituents. Phone callers were provided with a check-off list for each person they called.

If absolutely supporting Ms. Furse, they checked off a "Yes," and others were rated as "Indifferent" or "No." The "No" answers were never considered again.

On Election Day, they had people monitoring the polling places and checked off voters who voted for their party. They were compared to their master list, and if people had not voted by 5PM, volunteer callers started calling those who hadn't yet voted. These were the people who were already identified as supporters or swing voters. Of course, some people would not disclose their vote, but that's totally understandable.

They even offered senior citizens a ride to their nearest polling station, "It was literally person-to-person" effort to help people vote.

Ms. Furse won by the largest margin ever. Ms. Cross said, "It was a real adrenaline thing. Everyone worked long hours, seven days a week."

CHAPTER 10
The Candidate Must Show Up:

The campaign manager, along with the candidate's fundraiser, has to schedule fundraising events for the candidate to attend. They can be small events, such as coffee klatches, in a local diner or restaurant in the morning, senior centers in the afternoon, bars in the afternoon or evening, gala events, or receptions in private homes.

You really have to show up at all these venues and show the people that you're willing to come out and shake their hands. If you're running locally, most people who vote will know about you, and they'll have some opinion about you. If you're not there, you're more noticed than if you are. Richard Croce says you don't have to talk politics. All you have to say is 'Hi, I'm so and so and I'm running for [for instance] county judge. How ya doing? It's nice to meet you." And that's it, and they'll say, "Wow, so and so showed up at the fundraiser and he shook my hand!" This is an opportunity to positively influence people and change their opinions.

Candidates need a scheduler ["stage director"] who handles schedules and coordinates events, one who tells them where and when they must be. It could be a Kiwanis Club at 8AM on a Saturday morning, 9:30 at a senior center, 10:30 at a Synagogue, and Sunday morning the Bassett Church and Asian Society dinner Sunday evening; Knights of Columbus, Monday; LGBT center, Tuesday: Boy Scouts award ceremony, Wednesday; and so on. One must have a strong constitution for pounding the pavement, but that's how the votes come in.

Speaking of attending fairs and festivals: They are attended mostly by local people and families. Chances are your party will have rented a booth, for part of which I'd suggest you chip in, and that is an excellent place to practice your greetings and very short informative speeches of 15, 30, or 60 seconds. These are held very early in one's campaign, so even if you goof a little bit initially, practice makes perfect. By the time the heat of the campaign rolls around, you will have perfected your short speeches. Learn to keep them extremely short and down-to-earth pleasant. Hand out palm cards, fliers, buttons, balloons, bumper stickers, plastic shopping bags, or other catchy tchotchkes, all imprinted with your name, position and slogan for which you're running. **Learn how to shake hands properly.** It's in Chapter 18.

Parades: Get the schedules for firemen parades and 4th of July parade and get their permission to march in them, holding your banner, or permission to include your float in the parade, emblazoned with your photo, slogan and office for which you're running. That all makes a very large impression in front of hundreds or thousands of local residents.

Richard Mathews said that no matter how many events he would attend in a day, there would always be one person who would come up to him and tell him, "Man, you shoulda been at the American Legion over the weekend. They had seventy-five people there!" And I would ask, 'How many places can I do???' The thing is if you have a schedule of events you can look at, you could then pick and choose which ones you want to go to. I'm sure, knowing Mr. Mathews, that in that case, he wasn't aware of that event. If it was the American Legion, he would have never missed it. He's a true patriot.

The candidates are expected to attend and make a speech. Each speech must be tailored to the specific audience to some degree. It doesn't matter whether the event has 5 people, 126 or 348. The candidate **must** attend and cannot be AWOL, no matter how small the event. It looks and feels terribly bad if the candidate sends a substitute. **It is the worst thing a candidate can do.** Candidates, however busy, have to show up, even if they are flat in bed with the flu. People are not interested in hearing surrogates, and feel cheated and demeaned.

Candidates don't have to make long speeches and can explain that they must be at some other event shortly, with sincere apologies. People can expect that, but can be extremely resentful if they are left high and dry *sans* candidate and accompanying speech. I would think the result of this could affect the bottom vote line of the campaign.

Judge Anthony Kane never spoke for more than five minutes or so. He wrote his speeches out, although he said that he could easily speak extemporaneously for an occasion or events. But he always made notes in advance. For most speeches though, he always wrote them out. "I've seen too many speakers get off on tangents and five minutes runs into twenty minutes. I'm very conscious of that."

It is understood, through invitations, that **"Come Meet the Candidate"** events are fundraisers, and supporters are expected to bring checks and/or credit cards. If they're larger fundraising events, there would be an expected specified contribution for admittance.

Candidates also need endorsements from prominent public servants and prominent people in the community from one's Party, as well as one's party itself. Most of all, from newspapers, advocacy groups and labor unions, especially true in big population areas, like Portland. The groups and unions will provide campaign contributions and volunteers. Of course, unions will have to be reassured that they'll have your support, and in return, you will get their votes.

That's how it works, folks. Nuthin' for nuthin'. The groups and events to go after are teachers, police, firemen, women's groups, environmental groups, highway employees, other public employees, gun groups (if you support them),and unions. Candidates need to attend sporting events, grand openings, civic functions, festivals, fairs, Industrial plant and large business tours, as well as many others. You get the idea.

Do your homework:
Get the local (or national) newspapers to support the candidate. The best way is to arrange meetings with editorial boards who will subject the candidate to rigorous questioning. Anticipate as many questions as possible and practice the answers with your staff on all the key local issues. They're your brain trust. Preparation is critical.

You don't want to look stumped by not being able to answer the questions. Many candidates seem to have developed the *"End Run Technique"* by being evasive in either not wanting to answer a question or unable to provide a clear answer. It's almost an art, watching them squirm their way out of it. They're like running backs, twisting and turning, but good reporters will smell blood and tackle them down. Good looks are not everything. Sooner or later, an unprepared candidate will screw up and someone will yell, "The emperor isn't wearing any clothes!" and that candidate is headed for the "waste of money quicksand pit," never to get out.

Candidates have a responsibility to everyone on the team, as well as to those who've financially supported the campaign. They have to be "A" students.

"Why do connected people to the community lose? Maybe they do not have the charisma or do not inwardly want to win, or think they have no chance. Of course, if they want to win, but have a job and cannot devote 24/7 to the campaign, they do not have a chance.

"If you have the credentials and background, and are well known in the community, have a good platform and a good campaign manager, as incredibly time-consuming as it is, you will then have the best chance of winning.

"If you're new to the area and running against people who have roots in the community, you will, most likely, have no chance to beat them."
– Marcy Goulart, former President, Democratic Women, Ulster County, NY

Greg Helsmoortel has been the supervisor for the Township of Saugerties, NY, for eight terms! That is most astonishing, and I asked him what **his** magic is. "I think I'm respected, **I have roots in the community.** I've always been active in business prior to politics, sponsoring numerous events, and I was very well known that way. It was a civic duty and business, too, contributing to the community and making a living in the community, and I did that extensively, with no regrets."

"It takes stamina to have to run every two or four years. You have to work your way up and learn how to solve the problems of the county before trying to solve the problems of the state. Run for trustee or mayor for a first campaign or some lesser office. The arrogance is unbelievable when candidates try to run first for higher office. Most of time, they'll fail. Acquire experience and build up to the next office if you're that ambitious. You have to be patient and learn the machinery of government."
– Marcy Goulart, former President, Democratic Women, Ulster County, NY

You cannot let your ego get the best of you. Making friends with fellow lawmakers, trusting them and earning their trust of you is critical. Amiable friendships with your adversaries will be a major plus, as well, to your degree of legislative achievement. Master the give and take and compromises necessary for getting your agenda and programs into law. Of course, we all want it all, but sometimes we might have to settle for "half a loaf" at a time, or maybe even just a few slices. It's better than nothing, and next time, you'll get to add another slice or two.

Zig Ziglar, motivational speaker and author, said, "You can have everything in life you want, if you will just help enough other people get what they want." Makes sense to me.

"I think when you get to those special places where you're making major reforms, that makes the government significantly more able to serve the citizenry, while simultaneously not elevating property taxes, it puts you in a position where you have significant benefits to everyone. And that's really where it cuts across the boundaries between Democrats and Republicans and people who view themselves from all different parts of the far left or the far right in many of these different parties.

"I like to think of this as a collaborative approach with people on both sides of the aisle to focus on the bottom line, which is the people, and we've gotten, fortunately, enough support so that it worked itself off the board again. They're going to think of themselves of offering opportunities for all people. ...and in the end, sweeping changes have taken place, and this has been very effective."

"From that point, we showed a track record of success, and once you're able to show honor and integrity, you have the capacity to speak somewhere from the perspective of developing a level of trust on both sides of the aisle so that it's not going to be a highly politicized conversation, as much as going about what the best interests are of our citizens..."
– Michael P. Hein, County Executive, Ulster County, NY

If you're successful in that regard, be sure to include and compliment your adversaries and their contributions to the successful passing of your bills. It's a gracious thing to do. Don't be selfish. You'll be resented. Heap praise. Be humble.

"Change equals resistance. If and when resistance is overcome, change equals progress."
- Jeff Siegel, candidate for County Legislature, Sullivan County, NY

CHAPTER 11
OH, WHAT A BEAUTIFUL BABY!

The Birth of Your Platform and Your Kitchen Cabinet: What are the other issues of your campaign? These must be formulated and prioritized. In local political campaigns, you do not need a million issues. Simplicity will allow you to convey your issues much more strongly and repetitively. See what resonates the most with the public. Ask people what bothers them the most and take those issues on if you agree and feel you'll be able to do something for your constituents.

Set up a kitchen cabinet of friends and party officials and acquaint yourself with the most important issues. Candidates and Campaign managers should be reading as many local publications as possible in order to focus on each community's most pressing issues. Poughkeepsie Common Council Chairman Chris Petsas says, "I don't think people are worried about gun rights in my district, or abortion rights or other national issues. I just think that politics has to be local. You have to have a good platform that average people can relate to: Getting abandoned homes back on line, paving of our streets, fixing the sidewalks, fixing up the city parks. In other words, the things that really come home to people."

If, after speaking with numerous citizens, you decide to select a controversial issue or two that will alienate local voters, perhaps do so without your name on them, if you and your team all perceive that they will hurt the chance of your election.

On the other hand, there are some candidates who wear Teflon outfits, who can courageously talk openly about any touchy issue and get away with it, and are considered to be courageous and honest, and who command respect for not skirting those issues.

The question seems to be whether you're independent enough to voice those issues, or whether you're muzzled by special interest contributors and lobbyists. That money can seem so awfully sweet in influencing one's opinion.

"A really smart campaign person will come into an area and find the ten most influential persons working on a campaign to inform him or her of the issues. If they want to take the time and give respect to the local people, then the locals will work hand and hand with them. But if they come in your town, county or state, and tell people what to do who have already been working on a campaign, then hey, 'This is what we're going to do,' these local people will leave because they weren't given the respect they deserve. It happens all the time."
– Marcy Goulart, former President, Democratic Women, Ulster County, NY

When visiting those individual communities, draw up a list of those perceived issues and study them so citizens and officials can readily address them with you. You can also go into any local diner early in the morning where all the locals go, and ask pertinent questions about local problems/issues.

People will not hesitate to give their opinions. Look them directly in the eye and ask what they think. Be a good listener. It's key. Don't over-assert yourself and interrupt. All of this takes legwork and patience, but will handsomely pay off in the end. Don't be shy about introducing yourself. Strong handshakes count, BTW.

As a candidate, ysou have to try to reach as many people as possible. In congressional races, it is much more difficult to do so, and candidates have to use other means to communicate to everyone, such as social media, TV and radio commercials, billboards and newsworthy events. These could be dedication ceremonies, press conferences, interviews, chamber of commerce speeches, other speeches in pertinent places for discussing issues. You have to get your message out. That costs money that has to be raised in order to do it all effectively.

Congressman Chris Gibson said he "spent time listening. I would tour businesses, listen to business owners, listen to their employees, and the media would be there to cover it. I made myself available for interviews and for any questions to earn trust with the voters. You'd also earn the trust of the media.

"Too often, you see elected leaders trying to manage the media and sort of manipulate the media. I felt my role was to be accessible, because the media plays an important role in a free society, of reporting and providing that information. I got a lot of recognition and elevation of the campaign through hard work from all these various places I went, that, in many cases, the media covered. That was important."

There are two ways of talking to people and two ways of saying things: When running in local campaigns, stay away from voicing negative issues in negative terms. Make your negatives into positives. You don't have to say that, for example, the mayor is a terrible communicator. You could say "I would try to improve communications with elected officials and do what I could to try to solve issues with the Mayor." It really bums people out in local communities to speak in a negative way. Jeff Siegel, running for County Legislature in Sullivan County, NY, and his opponent Ira Steingart, were friends, had dinners together with their wives, and agreed to avoid negative campaigning.
They shook hands and their campaigns remained positive throughout.

It was simply better to advocate that one would make everyone's lives better, instead of denigrating the other candidate. It's quiet warfare and more civil. It's nothing like the presidential debates we've been watching. Local candidates don't talk about hand and penis size, which leaves me wondering if the guy with the biggest schlong will actually become our president? Mr. Steingart won.

"If people see you as too large, then they feel like they can't tell you anything."
– Marcy Goulart, former President, Democratic Women, Ulster County, NY

Think what can happen to your campaign if you don't listen

Chapter 12
JUDICIAL CAMPAIGNS HAVE TO TAKE THE HIGH ROAD

Some sample slogans:
"Proven Judicial Experience"
"A Family Man (or Woman) to The Family Court"
"Family Man, Community Man"
"Qualified   Respected   Experienced"
"Respected By Our Most Admired Leaders (Testimonials")
"Family Woman (Man), Experienced Attorney"

In America, the stature of the judiciary is sacrosanct and the laws are there to protect the citizenry from judicial corruption. Judges interpret the law and their behavior is expected to reflect the highest level of integrity in serving the public. That is universal, no matter what the court is, from local village judges all the way up to the Supreme Court. Local judges might not be actual lawyers, but they are expected to deal honestly with local grievances, and not judge their decisions by the people they might know. Of course, that's not how it always works, but generally, judges enjoy the reputation of blind justice and high legal standards applied to all, no matter whether rich or poor, race, sexual preference or original country of origin. Our judicial system is what makes America so highly respected internationally.

First things first: In remembrance of a master Listener-in-Chief:

The late Chief Judge of The New York Court of Appeals, the Hon. Lawrence H. Cooke, would walk into the Miss Monticello Diner in his hometown of Monticello, NY, in early mornings, wearing his wide straw hat, white shirt and tie, and start greeting most people in the diner by name, always with a Mr. or Mrs. in front of their last names, and ask about their businesses, farms, farm animals, children and personal celebrations or other family matters. He had a hearty laugh that came easily and his portly figure shook with merriment when he did so. I watched him in wonder at his extraordinary memory for names and his intense interest in everyone. I kept thinking how Lincolnesque he was in his sweet humility, gentle rapport and the respect he genuinely expressed to virtually everyone. He was loved and unbeatable, and the highest judge in New York State. In Monticello, they called out, "Hiya doin', Judge!" and he always greeted them back in his homespun, country, Roosevelt-sounding voice. It should be a lesson in civility for every public servant and candidate aspiring to higher office. He also raised fancy chickens in his spare time. Probably no doubt he was loved by his chickens, too. (Just wanted to throw that in.)

Judicial political campaigns (in New York State) are highly restricted in comparison to all other campaigns by necessity. Candidates are not permitted to criticize their opponents and are limited to only provide information about their own virtues and qualifications. As mentioned elsewhere in this book, every state has its own requirements for judicial candidates on the campaign trail.

Campaign strategist **Diana Spada** will only work for candidates in whom she believes. She will not bend and will never compromise her standards for supporting a candidate if that candidate didn't meet those standards for potential public service.

In this regard, she interviewed a judicial candidate for family court judge and asked her "Why do you want to do this?' I'm thinking in my head, she's 34, two terms, run one more time, 20 years, she'll retire out at $175K a year. You know this was in my head, and she looks at me and says, "I knew from the moment I graduated from law school, the first time I walked into family court, that that was what I was put on this earth to do."

I said, "Why do you say that?"

She said, "It's because I can help kids."

I said, "Oh, tell me about how you think you can make a change in family court.

"She started talking about a couple of changes she thought she'd be able to implement and I said that everyone always looks at fathers and not paying taxes or payments, will pay six months from now and they put out the bench warrants and who say they're out of work, and she said, 'That's not happening. It's not about fathers and mothers. It's about helping kids and if I find out that they're working under the table, I'm also going after the people who are paying them.'

"I pondered that awhile and that's an answer no one could've prepped her to say, because nobody would've known I was going to ask that question." Ms. Spada agreed to become her candidate's campaign strategist and as a result, and she won.

Judicial candidates are not permitted to endorse other candidates in any position, nor campaign for other candidates. At the time of this writing, Family Court Judge Anthony McGinty's wife, Sara, an attorney and former town judge, was running for Surrogate's Court judge. Prior to her decision to run for Surrogate's Court, Ms. McGinty served as her husband's campaign manager.

Now that she, herself, was running, Judge McGinty was **NOT** permitted to support or campaign for her. In our discussion, he was very firm and principled in this regard, and she had no such expectations, as well. **They are not even allowed to solicit contributions** or know who their contributors are and must set up bank accounts and websites to include credit card and check payments that are blind to them.

Finance Director/Treasurer Burt Gulnick, says, "It's strictly logistics where the person who's the treasurer is concerned. The judge makes **NO** decisions how that money is spent. There's a separate address, separate phone number. They can say, 'Please donate to my campaign,' but they personally cannot solicit.

"They cannot ask you in person. And what the judges do with the money they receive from that election cycle? They have to spend it all, and if they don't, they're supposed to return it proportionate to the donors. Judges' campaigns are a different animal."

Campaign manager Richard Croce said, "Standing judges are prohibited from endorsing or supporting any candidate for any office, and a judicial candidate cannot endorse any other candidate."

Judge McGinty states, "Judges are supposed to be non-political. We don't go to political events. We don't go to political fundraisers. We don't go to activities sponsored by a party, except in the period before and after our election."

Here is an exception: **RETIRED JUDGES have no such restrictions.** They are permitted to endorse their candidates of choice. If a judicial candidate is able to receive the endorsement of a retired judge, it is a major plus for his or her campaign.

At a fundraiser for a judicial candidate I recently photographed, the candidate for surrogate's court was actually endorsed by **four** retired judges, three of whom attended the event. Two of the three spoke to the audience on the candidate's behalf.

They also posed for photographs that would subsequently be used for the candidate's campaign, which made their appearance an even greater powerful statement of support, both verbally and visually.

Judge McGinty continues, "Judicial candidates are not permitted to speak negatively about their opponents, as well. It forces you to focus on things about yourself, your attributes. It forces you to sell people on you."

Judge Kane, in an interview with the editorial board of The Times Herald Record in Middletown, NY, was asked "'what my position was about things and I told them my position, and they asked me to make a comment about my opponent. I said I will not make a comment about my opponent. I'll tell you who I am. I'm not going to tell you who he is."

In a related discussion, I asked Judge Kane about his lawn signs and he answered, "No lawn signs per se. The only lawn signs were we'd take a poster and staple it and stick it into the ground. They didn't last very long. And we went around and never, ever, because I firmly believe that you didn't talk about the other guy, I never said anything about my opponent."

If one is running for a judicial office, the NYS *Judicial Campaign Ethics Handbook* is essential. It can be Googled. There are many laws and restrictions in the handbook that must be followed.

From *The New York State Judicial Campaign Ethics Handbook*:

The Committee has advised that "[a] judge who is seeking appointment or re-appointment to judicial office is not a 'candidate' (see 22 NYCRR 100.0[A]) and does not have a 'window period' of permissible political activity" (Opinion 14-30; see also Opinions 15-176; 96-97).

2.2.2 "**Window Period**" Defined. "**Window Period**" is an official term. The "window period" is the period during which judges and non-judges who seek an elective judicial office may engage in political activity pursuant to Section 100.5 of the Rules Governing Judicial Conduct (Opinion 96-29). There is no geographic limitation on permissible campaign activities during a candidate's window period (Opinions 06-152; 03-122; 95-109).

Calculating the start of the Window Period. The start of the window period for a particular elective judicial office is nine months before the primary election, judicial nominating convention, party caucus or other party meeting held to nominate candidates for that elective judicial office, or at which a committee or other organization may publicly solicit or support a candidate for that office (22 NYCRR 100.0[Q]).

Thus, to determine the start of the applicable window period, a judicial candidate may either count back nine months from the date of the formal nomination, i.e., the scheduled primary, nominating convention, or party caucus for that judicial office; or (if earlier) count back nine months from the date of an official party meeting at which a candidate for the judicial office will be designated and endorsed, even if that designation is subject to being contested at a subsequent primary; or (if earlier) the date of the commencement of the petition process for that judicial office (Opinions 07-152; 06-152; 05-97; 02-90; 94-97).

The Window Period, as mentioned above, is open nine months before the first date at which you can be formally nominated by the party in a county-wide election. Judges do not have to be affiliated with any party if they so choose to run independently. You can meet district leaders, fundraise, go to other peoples' fundraisers, go to political committees and engage in political activity during the **WINDOW PERIOD**, before being nominated and elected.

Essentially, the party convention is when you're nominated and then six months after the election, you're allowed to attend political events to say 'Thank you.'" Ms. McGinty says, "There are rules, which are all about preserving an appearance of impartiality of the position. You are not making policy and you have to look like you're open and fair and unbiased."

In the Township of Fallsburg, NY, lives a retired 80 year old town judge named Isaac "Yits" Kantrowitz from the tiny community of Woodridge, NY, a town of perhaps, if you stretch it, 900 people. He is known to everyone as "Yits." As far as anyone is concerned, the name Isaac doesn't exist. No one calls him that.

Yits owned a body repair shop in Fallsburg, NY, known as the best body shop in the entire area. Its reputation for excellence was unsurpassed. When he was younger, he lost an eye there while working. He eventually was fitted for a glass eye and throughout his entire life, he never hesitated to remove it for anyone, including his grandson, whose bar mitzvah cake he decided to decorate with it during the solemn candle lighting ceremony. He also surreptitiously dropped it into a friend's martini glass at a cocktail party.

Yits is one of those guys who is loved by all and enjoys the best reputation in the local community. It's where he grew up.

Years ago, he was asked to run for village justice of the peace by a local lawyer against a long-time incumbent. He agreed, had no petition, no committee, no literature. The incumbent had been in office for many years and was arrogant enough to think he could never lose and never bothered to campaign.

Yits's wife, Gloria, made phone calls to everyone in the village and knocked on every door, even in the back woods homes. It didn't matter what party. She knocked and knocked, and they beat the incumbent, who never ran again. Yits served as the village judge without ever again having an opponent to run against in that position.

He was then asked to fill in for the town judge in the Fallsburg Township and served for two years until he had to run for the office. He ran against the son of a prominent, local judge.

While Yits worked, Gloria again went knocking door to door and handed out fliers, posters, plastic shower caps, pencils and a **"Backseat Driver's License."**

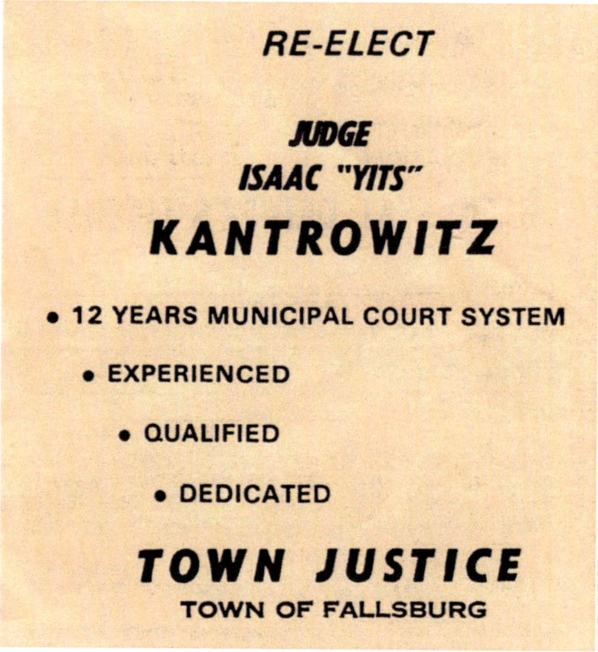

```
RE-ELECT
JUDGE
ISAAC "YITS"
KANTROWITZ

• 12 YEARS MUNICIPAL COURT SYSTEM
• EXPERIENCED
• QUALIFIED
• DEDICATED

TOWN JUSTICE
TOWN OF FALLSBURG
```
Front

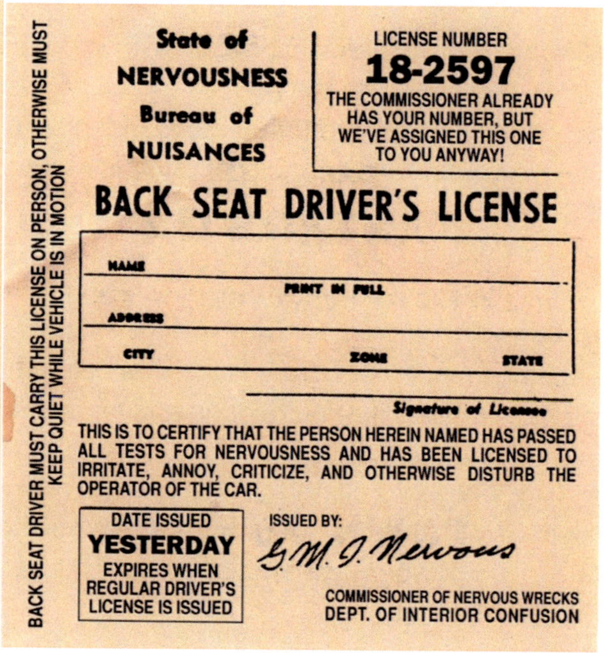

```
State of NERVOUSNESS
Bureau of NUISANCES

LICENSE NUMBER
18-2597
THE COMMISSIONER ALREADY HAS YOUR NUMBER, BUT WE'VE ASSIGNED THIS ONE TO YOU ANYWAY!

BACK SEAT DRIVER'S LICENSE

NAME _____ PRINT IN FULL
ADDRESS _____
CITY _____ ZONE _____ STATE _____
_____ Signature of Licensee

THIS IS TO CERTIFY THAT THE PERSON HEREIN NAMED HAS PASSED ALL TESTS FOR NERVOUSNESS AND HAS BEEN LICENSED TO IRRITATE, ANNOY, CRITICIZE, AND OTHERWISE DISTURB THE OPERATOR OF THE CAR.

DATE ISSUED
YESTERDAY
EXPIRES WHEN REGULAR DRIVER'S LICENSE IS ISSUED

ISSUED BY:
G.M.J. Nervous
COMMISSIONER OF NERVOUS WRECKS
DEPT. OF INTERIOR CONFUSION

BACK SEAT DRIVER MUST CARRY THIS LICENSE ON PERSON, OTHERWISE MUST KEEP QUIET WHILE VEHICLE IS IN MOTION
```
Back

It was a creative, grassroots campaign. Gloria and daughters stood in front of local post offices, and on weekends went to every barbecue, pancake breakfast, every other event anybody ever held. "It was fun!" she said.

Yits beat his opponent by a three to one margin. "Everybody loved him," said Ms. Kantrowitz. "He was funny. He wore a name pin. I have never met a lawyer who appeared in front of him who did not think he was the fairest judge, with common sense, and everybody loved to be in his court." In his case, it was said that although justice is blind, but in Yits's case, justice was truly only half-blind, and no one ever witnessed the removal of his glass eye while on the bench in court.

Gloria and Judge Yits Kantrowitz holding *"The Ten Commandments,"* presented to him by a local sign painter. When he was a young boy, Yits's brother accidentally sliced half Yits's finger off in a meat slicer. The photos in the background were taken by me of Yits in the act of…

Judge Kantrowitz, standing left, also "served" as a member of "Nixon's Dream Supreme Court" for The *National Lampoon photo*, also taken by me on assignment.
He is the only surviving member of "The Supreme Court."
The photo was taken at The Avon Lodge Hotel in Woodridge, NY.

Yits said, "For village justice, I served for eight or nine years and the rest as town justice. All together, I served thirty years. You do not have to be an attorney to be a local official of town justice or anything in between, except for the highest court in the state. In local elections, everyone knows each other and parties didn't matter. I couldn't have lost. I knew everybody. Roots are everything in the community. I knew them. They knew me. I really enjoyed it! I really enjoyed it!"

Judge Anthony McGinty, Ulster County, NY, mentioned the importance of being able to communicate by telling stories about issues in court from cases he adjudicated, without using names, of course, or identifying details. He told of his participation in helping to get families through a difficult part of their lives and moving toward a healthy and happy family situation. "You want to connect emotionally with people, and the way to do this is to tell stories about people you've known or met or connected with.

"I was conveying compassion, caring, decency and commitment. When you run for judge, you really cannot say a lot other than telling people that you would be fair and open minded. There aren't really issues when you run for judge. What you really have to do when you run for judge is to somehow convey to people what your character is."

He stated that he "went door to door, used billboards, TV and radio advertising" to get his message across.

Former Town Judge Sara McGinty, who served for two four-year terms, mentioned attending events and spoke to other candidates, asking them where they were going, and if Mr. and/or Ms. McGinty could join them. These would be fundraising events, charitable organizations, VFW dinners church dinners, etc.

Judge Sara McGinty said that "You can go to an event with another candidate running on your ticket, and if you're lucky, he or she will offer to introduce you, and if that person is local, all the better. It's important to go to all these festivals in local communities."

Judge Tony McGinty said, "Always have a button on your shirt or lapel so that people know you're a candidate, and if possible, walk with someone from the community, so they can introduce you, 'Hi, meet my friend, Tony, who's running for family court judge, and so on.'"

Sample Letter (edited) on fliers that was provided by one of my judicial interviewees

Dear _____County Voter,

The facts show that I am the only family court judge candidate with a long and continuing interest in serving _____County in the Family Court.

I am the only candidate who now and for the last ____years has been a law guardian in the Family Court. I am the candidate who now and over the past _____years has had an active family court law practice. I am the only candidate who is a member of the family law section of the New York State Bar Association.

I believe, because of this strong background, which no other candidate can match, I can best serve _____County as Family Court Judge. I have proven that I possess integrity, patience, legal expertise, and dedication to hard work and to the law.

I pledge to you that I will administer an efficient, professional, and compassionate Family Court. Please give me your support on Election Day, November ____.

Thank you,
Signed, not typed

This sample letter, of course, can be modified for use in any judicial campaign.

CHAPTER 13
VOLUNTEERS: YES, I CAN! YES, I CAN! YES, I CAN!

Volunteers volunteer because of their belief in your agenda and the party's philosophy, and a strong desire to defeat the other opposing candidates. The key ingredients are the number of volunteers you can round up and their commitment to getting you elected. They have to be ready and dedicated to giving their all on your behalf.

Jodi Longto, a volunteer, says that volunteers "have to be passionate, driven, and have to know the candidate and his or her background.

"I believe in my candidates. That's very important. I could never volunteer for anyone I didn't believe in. It's my own sense of integrity. I can support the party and party line, but would not work for anyone I didn't believe in."

As an organizer, Ms. Longto's special skills encompass the essentials for utilizing the talents of volunteers, scheduling phone calls and dividing those tasks among specially trained volunteers, for one. They are provided with a script from which to follow and have practice sessions on how to warmly address people. They have to be people persons over the phone.

Volunteers assist with scheduling duties and help select which events their candidate has to attend.

Volunteers are recruited through a candidate's website, colleges, friends and word of mouth. New York Congressman Chris Gibson created a position of volunteer director who was responsible for coordinating all volunteer activities. The volunteer director reports to the campaign director.

His volunteers were mostly recruited through his website and county offices, and his team had about one thousand members throughout his 19th New York District. The volunteer director and campaign manager would use a map of the Congressional District to mark out where most of the volunteer activity was. If it was lopsided in one particular county or township, volunteers would be sent to those other areas with inadequate coverage in order to provide better penetration.

They were then able to target an event in that area, or more, meeting with local leaders and scheduling the candidate's appearances, as well as additional volunteer activity. They would also try to inspire local residents to join the volunteer team.

In this way, Congressman Gibson enlisted a whole legion of enthusiastic volunteers in each county. Each county had a county coordinator who organized all volunteer activities and who reported back to the campaign's volunteer coordinator. Congressman Gibson said, "In many ways, some of these approaches are similar to the military. You would have an operational center to track and analyze information and try to derive good insight on what to do, based on that analysis."

This is particularly helpful when organizing volunteers for statewide, county or township campaigns. A map of volunteer activity is a minute-by-minute reading of what volunteers are doing and where they are located, and where they can be better utilized when necessary.

People with foreign language skills are especially valuable for one's campaign, both for phone calls and going one-on-one and knocking on doors in ethnic neighborhoods. Ethnic volunteers are invaluable for introducing candidates at their ethnic social events. People want to know who their candidate's friends are. Their talents make a tremendous difference for the success of a campaign and should not be wasted. They are respected and have the pulse of their communities to share with their favored candidates.

Local candidate schools are excellent sources of training of and information for new candidates. Numerous candidates organize their own training sessions for volunteers and staff, manned by professionals and other incumbents who readily share their experiences and advice.

Volunteers are encouraged to enlist at least five additional volunteers each and then have the new ones also try to enlist five of **their** friends. This gives candidates the ability to cover far more territory in their county, district, state, country. It also makes it physically easier for individual volunteers to carry out their tasks without having to travel long distances.

"I can't overemphasize enough getting a lot of volunteers, foot soldiers, because the wider the sweep they have to cover, the **less** they'll cover. If you would ask someone if they would cover your block and the next block, that works, so the size of the organization depends on the area you're going to be involved in. If you ask them to cover eight blocks, they will get too tired and do much less than expected of them.

"Your campaign manager would set up a grid on their map and that grid could be based on the number of volunteers you have, and would determine how much each volunteer would cover."
-Richard Mathews- former chairman, Ulster County, NY, Board of Legislators

If it's a wide area, the more volunteer boots on the ground, the better, so that volunteers are not killing themselves. Volunteers are encouraged, as Ms. Longto suggested, to enlist more of their friends so that each would only have to cover a much smaller area.

Mr. Mathews, the Ulster County, NY, County Legislator, had his volunteers **knock on every door** in each neighborhood, other than the homes of known opposition leaders. He knew where the "hot button" people lived and made sure his volunteers avoided their homes, as they were the "live wires" and he didn't want his volunteers "getting electrocuted."

For him, the name of the game, considering there were a great number of independent and swing voters, was to "blanket" the area with volunteers and palm cards. In any case, Mr. Mathews never lost an election. He was on the Board of Legislators for Ulster County, NY, for ten years and chairman for five.

College students are the best volunteers. High school, too, of course! We can't leave them out. They have the energy and total involvement, as well as computer skills to give candidates the edge. Political science students predominate. It's great for their experience and résumés for future work after college. They are perfect door knockers and help with organizing schedules, training sessions for new volunteers, displaying posters, compiling data banks and surveys. And that is critical! Most of all, they can manage websites, Facebook and all other social media.

Candidates and/or their campaign managers must give volunteers meaningful work to do. If you don't, you lose, and it must be substantive work, **not** grunt work that does not challenge their talent. Volunteers want to be excited to have accomplished their part in the goal of electing their chosen candidate. Volunteer assignments must be substantive, satisfying and acknowledged. If so, they will do anything for you. People **NEED** to be recognized. The worst thing you could do for a volunteer is not give them substantive work or direction and ignore what they have achieved on your behalf. A great leader can achieve miracles from the troops when paying attention to them. Give them "shout outs."

Besides Ms. Longto, much of this information is from a person (unnamed) who ran a city volunteer complaint board for many years. I was told that the first thing you have to do is train your volunteers. They have to learn a tremendous amount, and for her, they were mostly seniors who were retired or semi-retired and who had done substantive work in their careers. There are many college student interns involved, as well, especially on the big campaigns. Their passion and volunteer involvement can change the world. That opportunity cannot be trivialized.

Volunteer work for the campaign is critical: If volunteers do not know what to do but really want to help, hand out assignments and choose a supervisory person or persons to look after everyone and regularly check on their progress.

Mr. Croce took his candidates around, door to door, as well as his volunteers. He told the volunteers exactly what to do by giving them a list of the "most likely voters" and asked them to look at it very carefully, then highlighting the names of people they knew. These people could be from organizations they also belonged to or knew parents through their kids, or friends and neighbors. Volunteers were then expected to contact them on behalf of the candidate.

They were given a script that started with "Hi, this is (YOUR VOLUNTEER'S NAME) and I'm on the campaign committee for (NAME OF THE CANDIDATE) and I'm going to support him or her. He or she is a great candidate and I wish you would support her also." Then engage in the usual small talk.

"It's important, with the list, for volunteers to understand the differences of expectations. What I've tried to do in later campaigns… Different people come in and out. Not everybody attends all the meetings and you know you will call them up and they will do something else. They will put up lawn signs, put up the big signs, go to the post office and hand out stuff.

"I try to lay out the expectations at the beginning of the campaign without scaring anybody away, 'cause some people will say they didn't know it would be this way. 'cause it is a lot of work."

Some people enlist as volunteers as a social out. But everything is time-sensitive and organized by both the campaign manager and strategist, including the mailing of checks to suppliers. Ms. Spada was incredulous that some would come in and say, "Did ya order the pizza? Do you have the soda? Did ya make the coffee?" Ms. Spada would say, "Oh, my God, are you serious?"
That's all well and good, but there's so much work for volunteers to help get candidates elected. One candidate placed a bumper sticker on her desk one day that said, "Volunteers are Important People." How very true.

It is also most difficult to fire volunteers if they cannot fulfill their designated duties, and volunteer directors try never to do so. It's hurtful and embarrassing, and people really want to help their candidates. So if they don't work out in one area, try to direct them to another where their talents would be more compatible with their skills. There's too much at stake for languishing and not being productive. Because so much is at stake, It's either work at one's highest levels for your candidate or (etcetera, as they say) get off the pot.

But… everyone is replaceable. You want only those who will walk on water for you. I don't mean to sound tough, but campaigns are so high energy and so "to the moment," that it's essential that everyone pull their own weight.

Here are some guidelines and assignments for volunteers:

Nothing should be left to chance.
Older volunteers may find it easier making telephone calls, reminding people to vote, offering to provide transportation, writing letters and sending emails to prospective voters, and collecting personal data to be entered into data banks: In other words, doing tasks that are not physically demanding. Younger student volunteers can do the physical legwork: knocking on doors, handing out literature in homes and businesses, outside a post office, making handmade posters for rallies, posting posters and signs, placing signs in the ground, posting on Facebook, Twitter, other social media sites and updating the candidate's website.

Show Your to your volunteers: As a candidate, **NEVER** take anyone for granted!!! People are giving their time on your behalf. Show your appreciation **ALWAYS!!!** See them regularly, "speecherate" them with eloquent and florid praise, bring them food, pizza, tacos, burgers, fried chicken, liquid refreshments, snacks. Spend extra time with them in your (various) headquarters. Let them know how incredibly important they are to you in your quest to represent everyone in your community, state, association, union, school or country. Candidates should periodically take over a phone and answer it themselves for a while. That will immensely impress people.

Congressman Gibson, when visiting a village, always makes it a point to recognize a particular volunteer who was instrumental in setting up an event. In his speeches, he will always express his "deep, sincere gratitude to that individual for their work, followed by a handwritten note." He also publicly presents these volunteers with special military coins used for special occasions, as tokens of his sincere appreciation. This was a military custom of his during his days in service to our country.

Judge Anthony Kane of the New York State Supreme Court (now retired), always went from home to home after each campaign, presenting a symbolic, single red rose to **EVERY** female volunteer. He, too, wrote personal notes of gratitude to **ALL** his volunteers. "You definitely have to take care of your volunteers by thanking them. You must say 'Thank you,'"

Make volunteers feel like they're part of the family. If you have a spouse or significant other, bring him or her down to your headquarters and introduce everyone to that person, and to your kids, too. Bring your dog if you have a loveable one. Sounds crazy???? Sounds warm and fuzzy to me, especially to students, too.

You cannot take people for granted, especially your volunteers who are working their rear ends off for you.

Create a "Volunteer Appreciation Day" and honor your volunteers for the specific work they've done. Single each one out if it's a small group, with personal comments. It must be the right, heartfelt appreciation. **Their** appreciation to you is in the work you gave them. The other is social, and is fun, but that's not really part of it. It's the gesture of appreciation for their efforts that count the most.

"Volunteers are recognized with a volunteer appreciation luncheon or other. Candidates generally recognize and thank them, hosting lunch and pizza working meetings. Working conditions are good-- always in an office with all necessary supplies." Jodi Longto, volunteer supervisor

You need them. Hug them. Kiss them. Shake hands with them every time you see them. Make them feel loved, as they **DESERVE** to be, and you will have a loyal, dedicated bunch of followers who will go to any length to get you elected. Listen to their experiences and suggestions and frustrations intently, and modify where necessary. They all deserve certificates of appreciation with photos, which are wonderful mementos that will be cherished.

If you don't show your affection and interest in your people, you're screwed. Disgruntled people talk and walk and then talk some more to their best friends. You don't need bad word of mouth! You need **The Human Touch**.

Not On My Front Lawn! By the way, if you're going to have a volunteer place a poster or sign on someone's property, make sure that the volunteer first asks permission. Nothing pisses people off more when those things are taken for granted, even when one knows that particular homeowner or business owner is of the same party. They may **NOT** want your posters/signs defacing their property and landscaping, however supportive they may be. Extend the courtesy by asking permission.

Lawn signs in local elections are considered to be very effective advertising pieces. If one drives down a street and sees a dozen or so lawn signs for one particular candidate, it shows the extent of support for that candidate among neighbors. Seeing that support might be quite of great benefit in influencing one's vote.

CHAPTER 14
REACHING OUT & SWEATING THE SMALL STUFF

"It's the little details that are vital.
Little things make big things happen."
– Late UCLA Basketball Coach, John Wooden

A long-range strategy to achieve the ultimate goal:
You must have a good ground operation. You have to plan ahead, and that takes a lot of patience, but you'll be rewarded with a possible appointment to fill in a vacant office or the nomination to represent your party in an upcoming election.

Find out who the key players are and where they hang out for, let's say, breakfast every morning. Start going there and get acquainted with them over time. One assumes you're a good enough schmoozer to begin conversations with those you will ultimately recognize and who recognize you and who will get to know what you do for a living and how you contribute to the community. That's a critical element.

Go to town board or school board meetings and meet with local members. Ask many questions.

Sweating The small stuff: Get in touch with your own business and social organizations, political party groups, local church groups, hospitals, reading groups, knitting and quilting clubs, mahjong and bridge clubs, chambers of commerce, foundations, colleges, arts organizations, LGBT groups, senior citizen groups, VA groups, unions, Boy and Girl Scouts, private fundraising teas, other clubs and schools. Ask many questions. Try to get on the boards of some of the important organizations.

One assumes this is all very altruistic, as it should be, but it's also a means to an end for an ambitious future candidate. Let's be realistic about that.

The "Players" will eventually take notice and might then consider you for elected office. Do not think you can walk into a party committee, unknown, and expect the support of your party. You must pay your dues and earn their respect and support.

You need a plan: As **Richard Mathews** said "If you don't have a plan, you can't just not have talked to people for the ten years before and then start talking to them, because you'll then have a "'reputation.'" What you need are your connections, people who think highly of you and who don't think they're being used. You're not going to pull the wool over their eyes. They're a pretty smart bunch of power people and they can smell a bullshitter a mile away.

You have to earn their imprimatur and have them think of you for the future of their party when it comes to nominating candidates. Mr. Mathews's father always said that *"If you live in a community, you should participate in a community."* Mr. Mathews ultimately became chairman of The Ulster County, NY, Legislature, and served in that capacity for five years (1986-1991) and was a member of the legislature for a total of ten years. He then retired from public office and took the words of his late mother to heart, "Fish and politics begin to stink after three days." He felt that limits should be set.

He was president of Kiwanis for two years, president of The Ulster County Chamber of Commerce, chairman of the board of one of the local hospitals and commissioner of jurors for fifteen years.

Reach out, either by yourself or through your campaign manager, and offer to "meet and greet," visit and speak. If you have friends in any of those groups, have them invite you and introduce you to everyone when you arrive. *"Mary Jones, I want you to meet my good friend, Rich Smith. He's running for town supervisor."* It's more polite and respectful to use Mr. or Ms. as a salutation when responding, but more often than not, we end up using first names in less formal situations.

Chumming the water: If you're a stranger to particular groups in political or social situations, try to always have a local, familiar colleague in place at meetings and social events from their particular circle who can introduce you and chum the water on your behalf. It's so much easier for you if you're able to do so, rather than going in cold. People are then happy to meet you, listen to you, talk with you. This is a role for county chairmen and ward people, and well as friends in social organizations. And then your circle widens.

Anthony Kane, running for the first time, initially considered himself to be somewhat shy and reserved and felt most comfortable handing people a flier or palm card when meeting them. On one occasion, he had arranged, so he thought, for a local committeeman to meet him at a chicken barbecue in the local Grange Hall for an introduction to his constituents. He and his wife, Nancy, took a button from some other person's past campaign, covered it and wrote "Kane for Family Court Judge" on it. They got there in the rain, on time, and waited and waited…and waited for the committeeman to show up…but he didn't.

So he and Mrs. Kane finally walked in, looked at the long rows of tables of people eating chicken with their hands and simply walked out the door back to the car. He told Mrs. Kane he couldn't do this and she said, "Okay, we won't run if you don't want to do this." (Psychology involved here.)

He then walked back in and to the front of the room and said, "Excuse me, I don't want to interrupt your luncheon and I just wanted to introduce myself. My name's Anthony Kane. I'm running for family court judge in Sullivan County. I just wanted to let you know who I was. Thank you very much. Enjoy your lunch." He kept his hands behind him so he wouldn't have to shake hands with their greasy hands, not that those people had any desire to shake Mr. Kane's hand at that time.

"It was just a pleasantry. You didn't have enough time and didn't want to interrupt and they weren't there to listen to you. There were just eating and visiting with their friends." He left his literature behind. He was probably in that large room for no more than three minutes. It was his very first event and traumatic in a way, having been left high and dry by an irresponsible committeeman.

A skilled, experienced campaign manager should take you around and make sure you shake the hand of **every** district leader in the county and every county chairmen, if running for statewide office.

As a candidate, you have to do your own research and have a basic, intuitive sense of what you have to get done, and not leave it up to your surrogates. You have to learn whom you are comfortable with in talking to and who can be approached personally for campaign contributions.

It's certainly easier, though, if you have a skilled fundraiser on your staff, someone who is experienced in shaking pockets as well. It allows you to leave the anxiety at home.

Go around the room and shake hands with absolutely everyone. Do not leave anyone out. If you know the person, a hug or kiss is always appreciated. Make sure you act warmly toward everyone. Smile and laugh. We will go into the crucial intricacies of hugs, kisses and handshakes in Chapter 18.

Meeting local officials in EVERY community in one's district is critical for forming new supporters and friendships, which will be invaluable down the line. "We decided to visit every event we could throughout the county and we relied heavily on friends in many communities who were attuned to these upcoming events, and because of my prior efforts of meeting officials, I was able to effectively follow up, creating an entrée to the people running these events: pancake breakfasts, lunches, social clubs, like the Elks, VFW, for example, firehouses, religious groups, LGBT groups, country fairs, street fairs, everything. We also went to nursing homes, retirement communities and local college events. We reached out to as many constituents as possible."
-Elliott Auerbach, Comptroller, Ulster County, NY

If it's a small coffee klatch or tea gathering, don't come empty-handed. Even though it's political, bringing some pastries, a box of chocolates, flowers, a bottle of wine (for later) or other pertinent gift, would be greatly appreciated. Maybe I'm overstating this, but I never go to a person's home without something. I personally, just find it to be rude and ungrateful. When supporters are putting themselves out for you, an appreciative gift is a lovely, considerate thank you. It's better than being thought of as a "taker."

Build a personal data base: Bring someone with you who can help with handing out literature and volunteer sheets when attending all these events– if it's an appropriate time to do so. Let people know how much you would appreciate their help in your campaign. A volunteer sheet should have one's name, address, email, phone number(s) and local area in which one is most interested in helping. It should have a checklist of candidate's campaign needs: phone calls, writing, emailing, driving door to door, marketing, data collecting, speaking on a candidate's behalf, poll watcher, etc. The list should also include names of friends and colleagues who also may be interested in voluntary service.

CHAPTER 15
THE APHRODISIAC OF POWER

Charismatic candidates should not
forget a pack of breath fresheners and some facial tissue

Owning the room

There are those rare candidates who walk into a room and immediately own it. Eyes are directed to them. People are drawn to them. Their presence is magnetic. People have to have a piece, and immediately, are upon him or her, hugging, kissing, handshaking and/or handholding, almost a caress. They cannot get enough. It's a group adrenaline rush and the energy is most palpable.

Some of the candidates are known incumbent public servants, others hoping to get elected. The stars with the magic are an intangible lot. Some are incredibly good looking and that's obviously a major asset, and others have outsized personalities that draw people in equally. It's all astonishing to recognize and try to analyze what it is about them that draw the moths to their light. You have to be magnetic, energetic, hard working and disciplined, and if it isn't sensational looks, it has to be on personality and accessibility.

Swim or sink– But if you're unsure of yourself and are naturally shy, you must try to resolve that problem immediately. Think gregarious and courageous and be aware that the shortcoming of shyness must be overcome. If you think you cannot swim, throw yourself into the pool or have someone push you. They'll be there to prevent your drowning, but it's up to you to swim to the edge and haul yourself up. You can do it!

Be a schmoozer– Walk into that room, put a big smile on, wipe that sweat off your upper lip, make sure you have your nametag (if necessary) on your right side of jacket or blouse, and American flag or organization pin on your left, and jump in, shaking hands. People who might know you, will hug and kiss you. Be sure to pop a breath freshener into your mouth. Don't forget some facial tissue for a drippy nose or involuntary sneeze. Small talk will flow. Ask questions of them of how they are, etc. It gets easier by the second. Shake hands on one knee with small children and talk with them. Hold babies, air kiss them; tell their parents how beautiful they are. Flattery never hurt anyone. Thank individuals for coming and express your sincere gratitude.

Judge and Nancy Kane, when they ran the first time, brought their sons with them to some of their campaign events. "The boys were 10 and 8 and they were very cute. Everybody liked little kids. That was a good thing. We went to one hall and we walked in with Matthew and Tim and I thought this was great. We showed up in our Dodge station wagon. Once you got out of Sullivan County's big towns, fancy cars were a negative. ." It was exactly the advice given by strategist, Diana Spada.

Rich Croce's advice: "One of the biggest things there is, as a candidate, is being humble. Don't come off with puffery. Don't proclaim that '"I'm gonna solve this problem', and come off with arrogance."

It's body language, it's the spoken word, I think it's how you communicate with other people: you look them in the eye, or do you go ahead and talk about your accomplishments? Nobody really cares. They want to know what you're going to do for them if you get elected. There's a way to express your success without having to say it.

And the good candidates know how to do that. It's instinct. You don't even have to learn it, although it can be learned. A good politician like Congressman Chris Gibson, is not only a good politician, he's a good government elected official because he's the greatest example like that I can think of. He never talks above somebody. He can talk at the level of anybody he's talking to. He can talk to the president of the United States or he could talk to a farmer in Dutchess County, NY. He would be able to talk to any of them and capture and keep their attention, just because of his humble sweetness.

"I know in my heart that man is good, that what is right will always eventually triumph, and there is purpose and worth to each and every life."
President Ronald Reagan

CHAPTER 16
SECRET WEAPON #1

"**We had much less money than my opponent**, but I had the most invaluable secret weapon any candidate would ever be so lucky to have, besides a reliable car, and that is my incredible wife Judy, who envelops people with her beautiful smile, big hugs and huge likability factor.

She loves to campaign with me and is "the complete package: brains, beauty, supportive of my goals and eager to make a contribution to the betterment of our Ulster County. She's as dedicated as I am."
–Elliott Auerbach, comptroller, Ulster County, NY

"Kathy didn't want me to run, but stood behind my decision. She was more afraid of the potential bad things that could happen to my business. My situation was more unique than others, because my company, the Spencer Daniels Agency, extended to other counties and supported me more because Sullivan County residents and businesses didn't have as much money as other counties."
– Jeff Siegel, former county legislator candidate, Sullivan County, NY

"My wife is always with me: The social end of it, going to special events, is something she enjoys, such as banquets, bake sales, firehouse suppers and church dinners. That is a tremendous asset, definitely."
– Greg Helsmoortel, supervisor, Town of Saugerties, NY

"To be a political wife, you're a saint. You should be sainted to put up with that ego and the loneliness you have to endure."
– Marcy Goulart, former president, Democratic Women, Ulster County, NY

Being on the stump, the campaign trail, requires endless hours and perhaps days, away from home and one's family. It's lonely for everyone in the family and one must recognize this, despite the frenzied headiness of campaigning. So therefore, if at all possible, schedule time at home to be with your family and regenerate relationships with spouses, children, parents, significant others. Eat meals at home, read bedtime stories, drink wine, share experiences, make love and **then** get back to the business at hand. It'll anchor you for the personal moments that really matter and reinvigorate you for the long, endless road of campaigning ahead.

CHAPTER 17
SECRET WEAPON #2: SNOWBIRDS, COLLEGE STUDENTS & MILITARY; THEY VOTE, TOO, YA KNOW

Secret Weapon #2: Mail-in absentee ballots are critically important and can make **THE DIFFERENCE** between winning and losing an election. You must be aggressive in getting the information out to people who you perceive will not be able to show up at the voting station. Target your audience. **Absentee ballots are available from the board of elections.**

Board of Elections Sample Absentee Ballot, Ulster County, NY

Ulster County Absentee Ballot Application

Please Print Clearly & Mail To:
Ulster County Board of Elections
284 Wall Street
Kingston, NY 12401

For Board Use Only
Town/Dst:
Reg #:
Party:
Absentee Type: _____

BOE Initials: _____ / _____

Commissioners Initials
_____ / _____

1. Name:
Address:
Mailing:
City/state:

2. I am requesting, in good faith, an absentee ballot due to (check one reason):
- ☐ absence from Ulster County on election day
- ☐ temporary illness or physical disability
- ☐ permanent illness or physical disability
- ☐ duties related to primary care of one or more individuals who are ill or physically disabled
- ☐ patient or inmate in a Veterans' Administration Hospital
- ☐ detention in jail/prison, awaiting trial, awaiting action by a grand jury, or in prison for a conviction of a crime or offense which was not a felony

3. Absentee ballot requested for the following election(s) (Note: Application only valid thru 12/31 of the calendar year)
- ☐ Primary Election ONLY   ☐ General Election ONLY   ☐ Special Election ONLY

Only Complete the section below with Specified Dates if you are Applying for more than one Election.
- ☐ Any election held between these dates: absence begins: ___/___/___ absence ends ___/___/___

4. **Delivery of Primary Ballot (check one):**
- ☐ Deliver to me in person at the board of elections.
- ☐ I authorize (give name): _____ to pick up my ballot at the board of elections.
- ☐ Mail ballot to me at above address or at mailing address below:

_____
street no. street name   apt.   city   state   zip code

5. **Delivery of General Ballot (or Special) Election Ballot (check one):**
- ☐ Deliver to me in person at the board of elections.
- ☐ I authorize (give name): _____ to pick up my ballot at the board of elections.
- ☐ Mail ballot to me at above address or at mailing address below:

_____
street no. street name   apt.   city   state   zip code

6. **Applicant Must Sign or Mark Below**
I certify that I am a qualified and a registered (and for primary, enrolled) voter; and that the information in this application is true and correct and that this application will be accepted for all purposes as the equivalent of an affidavit and, if it contains a material false statement, shall subject me to the same penalties as if I had been duly sworn:

Today's Date: ___/___/___   Sign Here:_____   Date of Birth: ___/___/___

7. **Only Complete** - If applicant is unable to sign because of illness, physical disability or inability to read, the following statement must be executed: By my mark, duly witnessed hereunder, I hereby state that I am unable to sign my application for an absentee ballot without assistance because I am unable to write by reason of my illness or physical disability or because I am unable to read. I had made, or have the assistance in making, my mark in lieu of my signature. (No power of attorney or preprinted name stamps allowed.)

Date of Birth: ___/___/___   Name of Voter: _____

Today's Date: ___/___/___   Mark: _____

I, the undersigned, hereby certify that the above named voter affixed his or her mark to this application in my presence and I know him or her to be the person who affixed his or her mark to said application and understand that this statement will be accepted for all purposes as the equivalent of an affidavit and if it contains a material false statement, shall subject me to the same penalties as if I had been duly sworn.

_____   _____
(address of witness to mark)   (signature of witness to mark)

If you have additional questions or require further information refer to the instructions on the reverse side of this application.

As one can see, it is extremely easy to fill out.
Every absentee vote is of critical importance and can make the difference between victory or defeat in a close election.

Targets: "First, we sent out preliminary letters to military personnel, college students, people in nursing homes, second home owners in the South, (the "Snowbirds"), retirement communities and people who were planning vacations that would not afford them the opportunity of voting in person. Data was everything, both the party's and the data bank and spreadsheets we set up. Numbers count.

"In those mailings was information as to how to obtain an absentee ballot and specific information for filing. We offered to help anyone, and provided our phone numbers, as well as email addresses.

"We followed up, as well. When the results came in for my first race for county comptroller, I was sure I lost, but one of the officials would not accept the results, even though I seemed to be far behind. There were still 6000 absentee ballots to be counted. We spent almost three weeks counting them and when the final results were in, I won by a grand total of… 124 votes. We **KNEW** then how important absentee ballots were and we assiduously courted those voters.

"As a consequence, the results were overwhelmingly in our favor. I'm now serving my third term as County Comptroller, serving the public."
– Elliott Auerbach, comptroller, Ulster county, NY

The lesson is that absentee ballots are critical in very close races, and obviously, can make **THE DIFFERENCE** between winning and losing. If making speeches to seniors in senior citizen centers or to military personnel or college students, be sure to provide them with the address of local Board of Elections so that they can pick up their ballots.

If there's a big spread in your district along party lines (board of elections data), and most people will be voting along those lines, absentee ballots are not quite as important to the outcome. But providing information to targeted groups will certainly be helpful— just in case. If the minority party has an extremely popular candidate running for an important office, then absentee ballots are critical for the opposition.

CHAPTER 18
THE ABSOLUTE IMPORTANCE OF A PROPER HANDSHAKE, KISSES AND THE BIG SQUEEZE

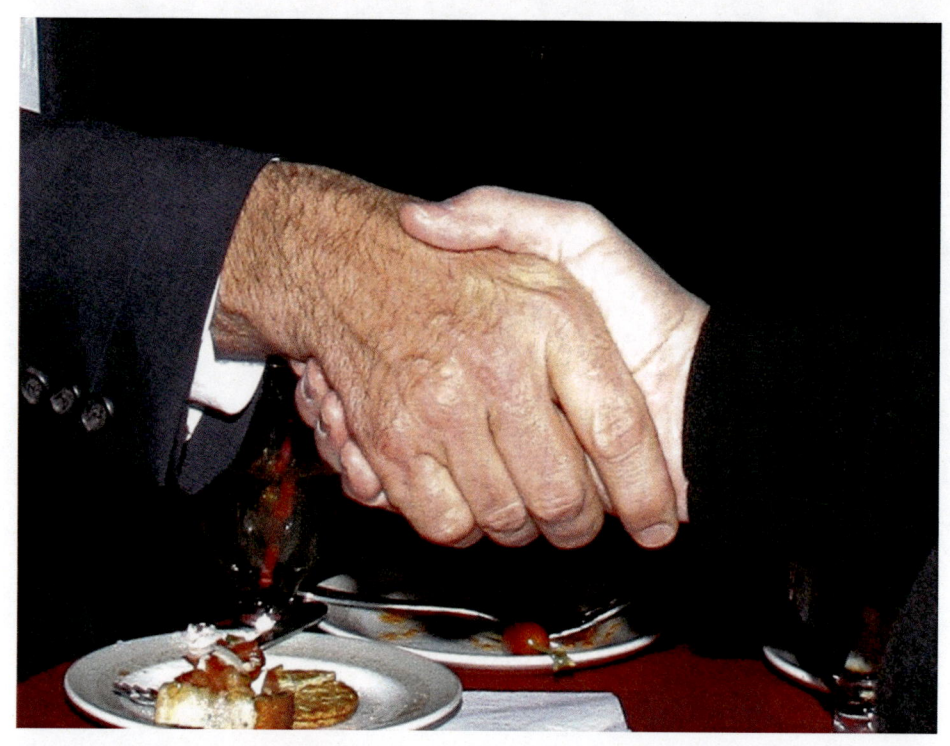

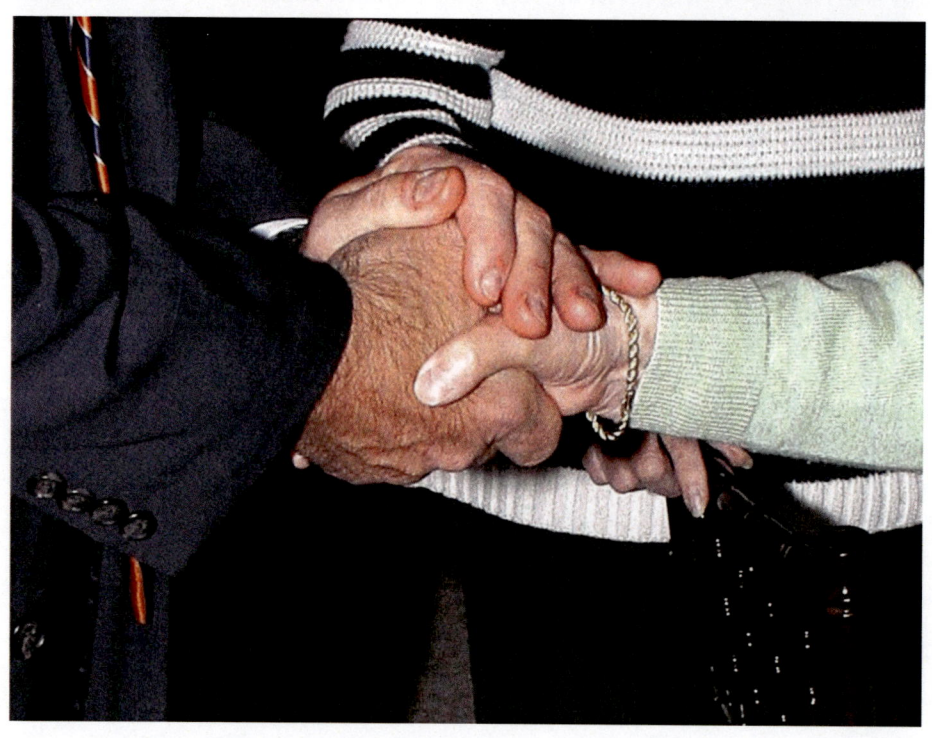

It's absolutely universal and basic. There is no substitute for shaking hands, for acknowledging people, for introductions, whether it be for presidential elections, gubernatorial races, senate, assembly, DA, supervisor, county executive, mayor, board of elections, college and high school races, union campaigns, social events, everything. We all shake hands. More so in smaller campaigns but, by necessity, less so in larger ones where the media assume a much larger role in introducing candidates.

Ed Koch, late mayor of New york City, was famous for standing at subway entrances during rush hours, shaking hands and asking people ***"How'm I doin'?"*** It was his famous phrase, almost his slogan. In New York City, the time-honored ritual of greeting people at 6am might be in Grand Central Station, Penn Station and other high trafficked locations. In any election, it's the "hit the bricks" technique, and is universal, even in Presidential campaigns, as well as for the primaries and state campaigns. Candidates in smaller communities shake hands in front of post offices, supermarkets, rallies, fundraisers, factories, office buildings, small businesses, outside of malls and other highly trafficked areas. You have to be relentless in "pressing the flesh."

When campaigning in front of stores or post offices, be sure to make your presence known to the store owners and postmasters and ask their permission, as a courtesy. Some store owners will ask you to please leave the area in front of their stores. If you continue to ignore them, you're asking for big trouble. They are quite capable of placing large signs in their windows opposing you and informing all their customers of their opposition. As for the post office, they cannot stop you, but it is simply a common courtesy to ask. And why make needless enemies, especially in smaller communities?

Judge Kane states, "You know it doesn't matter whether the person has any real say in whether you're going to be able to campaign outside their premises, the post office or even a place of business on a public street. You can stand on a public street and campaign, but you must, you have to go in and ask them permission whether you need it or not, and if they deny it, you have to go somewhere else. Even if you know you have the right to be there, don't do it, because people will always remember and talk about 'those' people who were discourteous. Always. You will get so much more bad publicity from a merchant who has the ability to communicate than you get from anybody else.

"And it's just, sometimes you just have to bite your tongue, but always, always, **always be courteous.** **That's a life lesson. That's not a campaign lesson, but a life lesson** and I guess if you're not that way, it's a struggle to be that way. If you're not a courteous person, don't run for office. You're gonna have a hard time."

Give people a firm handshake, but **NO CRUSHERS**. Those prove nothing other than your trying to prove how ridiculously macho you are. Why try to hurt someone? It makes no sense. If someone grabs your hand and you don't have a good grip, making you feel embarrassingly weak, grab their handshaking hand again, make an adjustment and tell them, "Now THAT'S better."

ALWAYS look at people in the eye. NEVER let yourself be distracted from that. It's a sign of rudeness and indifference. Spend that extra half second and look right at them. It's so incredibly important that you do so.

According to SUNY New Paltz Professor and Vice-President **Gerald Benjamin**, Governor Nelson Rockefeller made his handshakes legendary. They became known, as used in wrestling jargon, the "Half Nelson" and "Full Nelson" handshakes when he was on a receiving line. His favorite greeting was "Hiya, fella" (at least to men), and to expedite the greetings to constituents, he would apply one of those handshakes, depending on whether he knew those individuals or not. If he didn't know people, he would say, with his big smile, "Hiya, fella (or ma'am)", hold their forearms from underneath and give them a gentle push away so as to greet the next person on line. If he knew a particular person, he would, while shaking his or her hand, also say, "Hiya, fella (or ma'am)," place his left hand around that person's shoulder, give him or her a big personal greeting in acknowledgement, and only then would send that person on his or her way. It was both gracious, polite and expeditious by a master public servant.

Mwah! (the large kissing sound): Kissing discreetly, not romantically, is advisable. Kissing on the cheeks is prevalent, as well as the "French Kiss." Ahhhhhhhhh, you ask, what is the French Kiss? Might sound yummy, but NO, it's does not include the use of one's tongue. *Non, non, non, non, non!* Okay, it's also the European way of kissing and is most civilized. One would kiss the air next to both cheeks of the other person, not touching skin or makeup. "Hello, so and so," mwah, mwah. Sometimes, lips do come into play, but that's much less common. Do not forget to look into one's eyes. A hug usually accompanies those expressions of modest affection. Oh, and wipe that lipstick off when continuing.

And by the way, many women kiss women and men kiss each other, as well. It's common and most acceptable in certain circumstances. Perhaps that all depends upon the location and social culture one lives in, but I'm a straight guy and I have absolutely no problem with that.

The Big Squeeze— Hugging: Be discreet, especially if you're a man. Don't squeeze women too hard. You know what I mean. It can be embarrassing. As a political person, you don't want to be thought of as a lech. Hug professionally and keep the squeezes private. And one final suggestion:
Do keep your hands away from tushies, even if you think you can get away with it. **There are eyes everywhere and they're ALWAYS ON YOU**.

Do not ever let people see that you're looking at your watch in front of them. It's very rude! Do it most discreetly, turning away at a propitious time. This goes for your aides, as well. It makes people think you cannot wait to leave. Let your aides give you the time as a heads up to move on.

During those moments of meeting and greeting, many people will be taking photos, both candidly and posing with you. Cellphone selfies are ubiquitous and record those moments for people who will be able to say that they have photos of you and them together. Be gracious, patient, pleasant and practice your photo smile for the camera. I hate the word *"cheeeeese." So trite!* Remember to thank them.

You will also be asked for your autograph, and most often, a "selfie" with a constituent or two or more. Keep a Sharpie on you for autographs. Supporters want to remember you and you, in turn, should always remember who your friends are and who will help you get elected.

Keep that left hand free when shaking hands. Remember, too, that you should not be drinking during these events, even if non-alcoholic, unless the event is entirely private and the press is not present. It not only looks bad in photos and gives a poor impression. But if you're holding a drink, you will be prevented from shaking hands using both hands or handing out palm cards or business cards. This is especially true if you're attending business mixers. That goes doubly if holding a plate of hors d'oeuvres in one hand and a drink in the other. If you are holding a glass of wine, though, the proper, sophisticated way to hold it is by the stem and never holding the bowl.

BTW, as an aside: **Dr. Fred Mayo**, my co-author of our book, *Modern American Manners: Dining Etiquette for Hosts and Guests* mentions that if one goes out to dinner and drinks are served, the best way to handle the effects of alcohol is to eat a peanut butter and jelly sandwich with a glass of milk before leaving the house. It coats one's stomach.

"Yeadshd, it isha deljshfsahthfeh." Speaking of hors d'oeuvres, only eat the little ones. Too awkward eating small lamb chops and larger pieces. Doesn't look good when someone jumps in your face and your mouth is stuffed with the end of a bone or other food. Take small bites v. totally stuffing your mouth at public events.

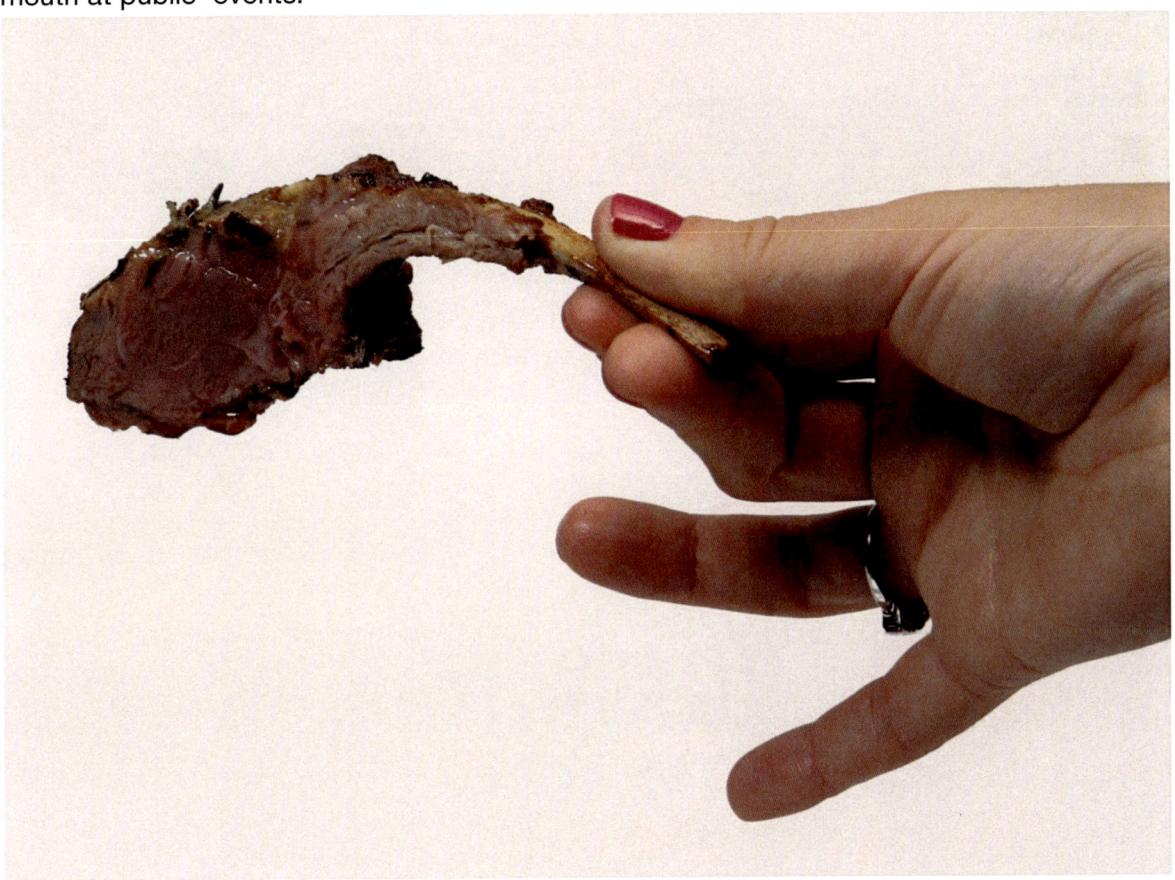

It's like the server in a restaurant who always manages to return to the table at just the "right" time, asking that horrible question while your mouth is totally full, "Is everything all right?" 'Yeadshd, it isha deljshfsahthfeh.' So embarrassing! Why are they even trained to do so???? A really good restaurant would never have their staff bother people that way.

CHAPTER 19
EAT FISH/DON'T EAT FISH: THE GREAT DEBATE

If you're going to eat at an event and must leave early, **Professor Gerald Benjamin** of SUNY New Paltz, mentionsed Louis Lefkowitz, the colorful past attorney general for New York State for twenty-two years, who said that one should then **eat a fish dish.** It generally came out before the other entrées, portions were smaller, and thus, gave the candidate the flexibility of leaving early, graciously.

Very old Louie Lefkowitz campaign pin found in an antique shop

On the other hand, **Marcy Goulart**, former president of Democratic Women in Ulster County, NY, tells candidates, **"Don't eat seafood! Never eat seafood!** You can get sick to death and be out of commission for four days. No fish! When you sit down to eat, you don't eat anyway. Push the food around. Eat a peanut butter sandwich beforehand and eat after you leave, at a diner or restaurant."

CHAPTER 20
POLITICAL PHEROMONES

Being loved is intoxicating. It is the candidates' political pheromone. The more loved you are, the more you want, and the more adulation you get, the more confident you become. It's the perception of power flowing through you. It's infectious and constituents are enthuslastically attracted to you. That is not a bad thing, but don't mess it up with careless behavior. Always be *"en garde."*

But... "You have to be able to "share the wealth,"' said **Richard Mathews**, past Ulster County, NY, legislature chairman. If a politician in power is invited to a special event of some organization, be it veterans or Office for the Aging, or social organizations, and an official proclamation was called for, he or she might ask another fellow legislator to go in his stead. It would mean giving that substitute legislator the recognition from an appreciative group of people so that the person substituting would get the credit for the passing of a bill, new funding, new facilities, honoring a special person in that organization, etc. **THAT** is "sharing the wealth" and playing good politics.

Mr. Mathews said that "It takes a village. You have to be humble and spread it around." One cannot allow one's ego to get too large and make fellow legislators envious. Success has many parents, and these "parents" will show their support when the next election comes around. Resentment is a powerful emotion, and being aware of the political sensitivities to the political pheromones of colleagues will be a plus to your future success.

You can't hog it all and be successful

Mr. Hein states that he does not come "with any sense of individual pride of authorship" when there is success in programs and bills that have been passed with the collaboration and support of the board of legislators. 'It's not a matter of me crossing the finish line. It's how many you can bring across the finish line with you. That's a very important concept for me."

Fred Mayo states, "I've always felt it is absolutely necessary to compliment one's colleagues as much as possible to make them feel that much better about themselves, as well as their feelings toward you.

"Politicians have to meet and greet people warmly and intentionally, showing the individual that they care, even if the interchange is only for a short period of time. They have to remember names or, at least, faces. They have to be gracious at all times and in all situations, and they need to listen to other people's causes and needs instead of always focusing on their own agendas. Basically, they need to pay attention to all the people at an event, often an exhausting task, but a critical one."
– Frederic Mayo, NYU clinical professor of hospitality and tourism management, excerpted from his and Michael Gold's book, *Modern American Manners: Dining Etiquette for Hosts and Guests*

CHAPTER 21
WHERE'S THE CANDIDATE? CAN'T SEE HIM OR HER. WHAT'D HE SAY?

Preparing to speak

I cannot begin to tell you how many speeches I've witnessed in which the candidate is in the same darkness as the rest of the people in the room, the only lighting of which coming from that little lamp on the podium. It makes the speaker look like he or she is in a horror movie, with the lighting from below. Try that with a flashlight, looking in the mirror to see what I mean. You should never present yourself that way! It's so incredibly unflattering, especially for women. Lighting is critical and theatrical. Don't minimize its importance.

Survey the room in advance, and if it's in a large space, ascertain whether or not the room is equipped with a spotlight toward the podium. If not, perhaps the event people can rig a spot bulb from the ceiling onto the podium. If not, try to get your own and plug it in from a short distance away.
Raise it up so that it's not blinding (if allowed to do so). That light will change the way people pay attention to you. You're the star of the show, not the ugly monster about to attack in the middle of the night.

You can easily find aluminum reflectors in a hardware or lighting store or specialized supply store. Light stands are available where photo supplies are sold. One that rises to 8'-12' would be ideal. Tape the stand to the floor so it doesn't topple over. If there's a column in the vicinity, place the light stand next to it and tie or tape it to the column. Safety first.

ALWAYS use a mic, even if you think your natural voice will carry. Your voice does not carry to the sides of the room, and if you turn your head to address one side of the crowd, the other side will be straining to hear you. Bring your own portable address system if necessary. You're not doing yourself any favors by being arrogant enough to think you don't need a mic. Mics are your best friends, as are spotlights. Speak into the mic and keep it close to your mouth, but not too close, as your voice will then sound muffled.

Try to videotape every speech and make excerpts of events, especially your interaction with attendees. These would make excellent clips, actually no-cost ads, on the various media sites, such as Facebook and YouTube.

Love your audience. Don't neglect your audience and various individuals throughout the audience. If you're not sure when to look up, notate the places on your prepared speech. People will be that much more attentive when you're looking at them. Do not bob your head too much when speaking. Keep it steady.

Speak with sincerity, warmth and intelligence. Appropriate jokes are appreciated. The late Chief Judge of the New York Court of Appeals, the Honorable Lawrence H. Cooke, once told me that he always began his speeches with a joke to gain his audience's immediate attention. He was a great orator and communicator and this is an excellent technique to immediately get an audience's attention.

Do not forget to mention the important people in the organization, as well as elected officials, and extend a special thank you to the person or persons who invited you, at the beginning of every address.

Make sure you've researched the specific important issues for each group of people so that you can knowledgably talk about them during question and answer sessions after your speeches. Thank them for inviting you, and let them know how special they are, no matter what the group. Also let them know that you're available for any occasion to introduce yourself and speak in front of them in the future, at the end of your speech. "It's been a privilege being here with you and I'll look forward to speaking to you again. Thank you."

CHAPTER 22
THE BOY SCOUT MOTTO, "BE PREPARED," PLUS A LOT MORE

Make yourself available to the local press: Newspapers, TV stations, radio stations, influential reporters and editors. Inform the press of your every public event and public meeting. Public events could be speeches to groups, meeting and greeting at local fairs and parades, patriotic holiday events and events unique to each community, debates, press conferences, dedications, award ceremonies, chambers of commerce, public safety, controversial occasions, school assemblies, locations of contested public issues, etc.

The Boy Scouts tell you to **be prepared**. How true. Do your **research and practice answers** to potentially sticky questions on controversial or mundane issues that will come up at town or village hall gatherings, community center events, fairs, at the end of speeches or from reporters. Make a list of what you perceive those issues to be and work out answers in advance. Your team will be most helpful in this regard.

129

Stand up at a podium, real or otherwise, and give your staff the opportunity to pepper you with tough questions, all of which you have to answer. If you're not prepared, you can put yourself in the position of losing an election, even if the polls tell you you've been ahead.

Practice some zingers of answers and responses to issues you know your opponent will bring up. These could be about personal slights, derogatory comments, insults, corruption charges, tax evasion charges, lies, diversionary and inflated expenses, accusations of racism, sexual dalliances, secret funds and bribery, equal pay, abortion, gay rights, lack of attention to infrastructure needs, emergency preparedness, beautification, high taxes, stop and frisk, needless public expenditures, crime and other local issues.

In this day and age, everything seems to be on the table. Nothing is sacred, and opposing candidates will bring things up that have absolutely nothing to do with your qualifications of being elected to the office for which you're running. Try not to interrupt your opponent(s). Better to let them speak. You will get your chance to pounce on their statements, but **do not let them interrupt you. Stand your ground and do not give in to their attempts to dominate you.** Interrupting is rude and is a turnoff to the public. It's also a sign of their inadequacy by trying to not let you clearly speak out. Do what you can to get the last word. **Call them out** on it if you have to.

You don't want to have a meltdown in front of the public. That will almost certainly finish you and you will go back into your bedroom and slap yourself on the side of your head for not being able to answer those pointed questions and statements at the spur of the moment, and you'll sweat all night long in humiliation.

Practicing and perfecting your answers can be the key to victory and your becoming a winning master debater. Be strong, be smart, be the alpha.

When **Susan Zimet** first ran for New Paltz, NY town supervisor, she and her husband/campaign manager **Steve Auerbach, wrote a different ad every week** in the *Hugeunot Herald* on issues that impacted the community, expressing her views on economic development, taxes, garbage industry, etc. The ads were titled "Town Matters" and were comprehensive position papers that people could easily understand. **This is a highly effective means** of getting a candidate's message across, as it looks more like an article than an ad. Placing articles in weekly papers is a powerful way to advertise.

The **Zimet/Auerbach** couple invested their own money in the campaign and two weeks before the election, the largest paper in the region wrote an article about her, stating "Two months ago, it was 'Susan Who?' and now it's become the most watched election in the Hudson Valley."

Ms. Zimet's slogan was 'SAVE OUR COMMUNITY.' Storekeepers in the community were universally against a huge retail box store being built, fearful that it would destroy the local, economic base of the township. One week before the election, **Ms. Zimet** placed (with permission) bright yellow posters in every storefront, proclaiming *"NO MEGAMALL. ELECT ZIMET."* She went on to win that election and subsequently prevented the giant retail store from building in New Paltz, the first town in New York State to deny that chain store a new location. Politics on a local level is very personal and voters came through for her.

That was **Ms. Zimet's** first campaign. She was town supervisor for the next four years and then elected county legislator for eight years. The leaders of both the Democrats and Republicans brought her back to run again and she won another four-year term for town supervisor. She served in these capacities from 1995 to 2016. She always worked across party lines, because as she stated, the issues were more important to her than the politics. She ran for State Senate as well, but had no chance against an entrenched incumbent. She knew it, but was heroic enough to still make a go of it.

Draymond Green, Golden State Warriors basketball player, said in a *New York Times* article that "The one thing we all hate in life is uncertainty. Whether that's in a relationship, whether that's in school, whether that's knowing what's being cooked, we hate uncertainty in life as humans."

It's your job to eliminate all the uncertainties you can think of by preparing and anticipating all those questions that will be tossed at you when being interviewed by the press or by constituents. Your answers have to go through the net every time. Two pointers are good. Three pointers are better. Three pointers win games and elections (and championships).

Remember that you are also there to LISTEN to people during question and answer periods. Answer questions to the best of your ability and make a point of getting back to people from whom you didn't have answers.

"If you're an incumbent and being judged and criticized on past mistaken decisions, own up to those legitimate criticisms and readily admit you've made a mistake in judgment, if that is the case. You can say you're trying to remedy that. Your directness and honesty, without hemming and hawing and weaseling your way out of it, will have a extremely positive effect on voters. As they say, "'Be a man.'" (Women included.)
-Richard Mathews, legislature chairman (retired), Ulster Commissioner of Jurors and chairman of Alternatives To Incarceration Program Board, Ulster County, NY,

If, too, you've come out on the "other" side of a controversial issue contrary to a group's feelings, be absolutely **BRAVE**, take a stand and stick to your guns if you truly believe that what you've supported is right. You're going to have to defend yourself, so be prepared with your logical arguments.
Fight for what is right, I mean, correct, but show total respect and patience for opposing views from constituents. But don't cave in.

"I do not agree with what you have to say,
but I'll defend to the death your right to say it."
That is Democracy.
– Evelyn Beatrice Hall

CHAPTER 23
NEGATIVE CAMPAIGNING

Negative campaigning is a vivid reality and one sees and hears it in greater and greater volume. It's not my cup of tea, and as one of my interviewees says, **"One should always take the high road."** It's exactly what my late and wonderful father-in-law always drummed into me, as well. His voice rings in my ears every moment I think of him and it's the best advice I could share with you.

"Kill'em in the crib" is a phrase used when the opposing party perceives an up and coming candidate making waves and starting to make moves to achieve higher office. The opposition will do everything it can to short circuit that candidate's ascent.

It could be negative campaigning, references to past decisions and endeavors, relationships with shady characters, possibly long-hidden skeletons, sexual escapades, financial irregularities or any other glob of mud that can be thrown. As I mentioned before, if you're thinking of running for office, better to divulge any potential problems in advance to save you the embarrassment afterward.

Oy, dirty politics... Sometimes, you just have to duck when you-know-what is thrown at you. But don't you be the hitter!!! "cause it'll be "One, two, three strikes, **YOU'LL** be out at the old ball game!" I'm incredulous at what I've heard during the last presidential campaign, with the bar mostly set so low. It's despicable and I hope you, as a candidate, out of desperation, will not stoop and lower yourself in the same manner.

The presidential campaign. What a mess it was! Un#$!#F%$%#$%believable!!! There has never been anything like this in my lifetime: The lies, dirt, demagoguery, anger, confrontation, acceptance of violence, racism, religious and ethnic hatred, email hacking, death threats, women-hating, innuendoes, physical inadequacies of little hands, internet lies, that face, getting schlonged, groped, Mexican "rapists," big walls, locker room talk, bitch, immigrants kept out, menstruation, jail threats, yelling, demeaning, insulting, debasing, punishment for abortions, threats of riots, nasty----and **MORE**.

Cathy LaBuda angrily says, "I was the first woman to chair the DPW and was told at some point that employees were stealing from the county. After a long and thorough investigation, two DPW workers went to jail. They stole thousands of dollars from the taxpayers. For example, they would purchase two of each of the items: stoves, refrigerators, lawn mowers etc., for the county and have the extra ones sent to their homes. They even tried to blackmail me into stopping the investigation since I was the chairman of that (DPW) committee.

"The following year, I was honored by the Sullivan County Peace and Justice Organization for rooting out corruption in the county, and the wrongdoers went to jail because of me."

Talking about dirty politics, Ms. LaBuda's opponent, she claims, lied about her and claimed **she**, in fact, was corrupt.

"To say *I* was corrupt was just over the top, and the opposition lied because I was one of the most powerful legislators, and they, my opponent, wanted to 'take me out,' for want of a better word, and so they lied about me. Really nasty stuff."

"We just need to rid the bad apples, the not so good apples within the committees, within elective office. We just want people to do the right things for the right reasons. I'm at the point now where I can talk, communicate with anybody under any circumstances. Believe me, I can, and I work very hard trying to do that, but those other people cannot. They just can't. **Some people are in office just to get the elected officials they dislike. That's all they do. If they can't do the right thing for the right reasons, they don't belong in elective office.** Fortunately, there aren't so many of them, but it's enough to make a difference."
-Frank Cardinale, chair, Ulster County, NY, Democratic party

Of course, if your criticisms of your opponents are true, by all means expose those **FACTS** to the public. The public has a right to know and you want to rightfully inform them and influence them to vote for you and win your election.

BUT…whispering is RUDE and those who engage in negative, lying campaigning dig dirt, plant (whisper) seeds and sow doubt, and then try to stab their opponents in the back. If you're in a small community, don't let anyone know it's you, though, doing the "farming." Unfortunately, a whisper campaign through other supporters is effective. Doesn't sound good, but that's reality about "the bigger the lie, etc." You have to be prepared to combat them.

Negative campaigning and ads will affect voters who are on the fence, the swing voters, considerably more so than those enrolled in the major parties and who are truly committed to their party's candidates. Those ads can be highly effective.

The theme of "Do unto others better than they could do unto you," is their New Golden Rule. Dispensing dirty, negative information is abhorrent, and diligent, intelligent voters will hopefully make one pay the price for that.

POWER F&%$@#G: I had never heard of this term, but apparently it's well-known in the political world, as I had been informed while writing this book. **Naïve me! Innocent, little country boy!**

Power men and women attract the opposite sex, and perhaps, the same sex, like a candle attracts moths. People who exude power, good looking or not, are attractors and experience the sexual heat from those who would like to have sex with them. They're the trophy politicians, the lions and tigers, the alpha males and females, who think they can get anything they want.

I'm told it's a lonely world away from home and things happen. I don't really give a damn what anyone chooses to do, but I'd suggest that one should be extremely careful in doing so. I'm not playing morality cop and I'm not being judgmental. What politicians do privately is their own personal business, but the repercussions can be deadly to one's political career as well as family life, if caught jumping into the cauldron of boiling turmoil.

Be aware that everyone has smartphones, Facebook, Twitter, YouTube, email, Instagram, Pinterest, etc. Be aware that surveillance cameras are everywhere, indoors and out. Be aware that wireless cameras can be about the size of pinheads and inserted anywhere in rooms, purses, briefcases, clothing. Try to find the backup cameras on your car, if you have them, and then realize that cameras are made much smaller than those. Look at your iPad or computer for the camera lens; it's tiny. Be aware that wireless microphones, too, can be placed anywhere in any innocuous place and voices can be recorded. Be aware that people can be planted just to trip you up in compromising situations. Be aware of whisperers who would spread the dirt faster than the Ebola or Zika viruses.

Be aware that the embarrassment factor and humiliation one would suffer could mean the political end for you. Do what you want, but If so, diligently watch your ass…and don't get caught with your pants down. It would be smart to be paranoid and extra careful.

From one of my interviewees, I heard of one western state senator whose wife found out about an affair he was having with an aide. He then had the task of retrieving all his clothes and underwear that had been strewn about all over the steps of that state's capitol building. The locks were changed and the car disappeared. Not sure about his re-election, but he did lose the marriage.

A Power@#$^#$!@$#%%$%$# headstone. R.I.P.

CHAPTER 24
WHO'S THAT KNOCKIN' AT MY DOOR?

The key to the kingdomPhoto: Burt M. gold

"So local politics? Knocking on doors. Number one. There is no substitute for it. There just isn't, and you can have somebody follow up, a surrogate for you and maybe go out and follow up later, but they **need** to know who you are. That's how important it is, and that's just grassroots politics. That's really what it is.

"People aren't going to vote for you if they don't know who you are. There are people, all things being equal, who will go across the republican line or the Democratic line, but if they know you and feel good about you, then they will make an effort and come out and vote for you."
-**Frank Cardinale,** chairman, Democratic party, Ulster County, NY

The ultimate object of one's campaign is to build momentum, one voter at a time, if necessary. Impress one voter, either positively or negatively, and he or she will mention you to other friends and neighbors, interjecting of course their feelings.

Knock, knock. *"Who's that knockin' at my door?"*– **It is most important to go door to door, knocking on doors until your knuckles are bloody**, handing out material and saying hello to everyone in the neighborhood. If you live in the neighborhood, all the better, especially if people know you as their neighbor. They will trust you. You must do the legwork and go to every targeted home you can. Do that more than once. Fellow neighbors talk. They'll remember and appreciate that you stopped by.

Writing in 1987, following his election to his town board in New Paltz, NY, humor columnist, **Mark Sherman**, had this to say in a political article he titled *"I'm In the Middle of a Dog."*

"**I have just had one of life's more unusual experiences**. I have campaigned for political office and, thanks to the people who helped me and voted for me, I won. But even if I had lost, campaigning provided many interesting experiences, of which perhaps the most interesting was going door-to-door.

"When I started the campaign, everyone told me that going door-to-door was the key to winning. I'm not sure how they knew this, but whether it was a councilman, a congressman or a book, they all said the same thing: The key is to go out and meet people.

"…As I campaigned this year, my friend pointed to one house and said, 'We'll avoid that one. There are two pit bulls there.

"She took me to houses she knew. We came to one of them, and the man who came to the door seemed quite rushed. "I'd like to talk to you," he said, "but I'm in the middle of a dog." As we left, my friend explained that he groomed dogs, and was in the middle of grooming.

"**… Do I think that going door-to-door is the secret of a successful campaign?** I don't know, but it certainly beats standing in front of ShopRite. People were pleasant enough there, but they were always in a rush, and about four out of five didn't live in New Paltz. Also, it was too predictable. At ShopRite no one was ever in the middle of a dog."

First, make sure you have a name tag, pin or special logo polo or tee shirt selected by the candidate or campaign committee, identifying the candidate- and you. These are your uniforms. Many respectable businesses have their employees wear uniforms. Uniforms separate you, and immediately identify you as being more trustworthy. You'll be much more readily accepted if you present yourself well. It is of the utmost importance that a candidate be seen knocking on doors, especially in smaller communities. People need to see you. Introductory handshakes with eyes directly on the homeowner is a major plus. Nothing like a sincere compliment about one's house and/or landscaping, or dog, as well.

Dress appropriately and casually professional. Create the best impression so that people will not automatically shut their doors in your face. You have to look presentable.

139

You cannot just knock on a door and be unprepared. You have to have an opening introduction and you want to create a dialogue between you and the prospective voter. People need to be enthused by you and you may have to walk that "extra Mile" to get to people in the backwoods. One candidate walked over two hundred yards to a house in the woods and that person exclaimed that, "No one ever took the time to come back to my house and talk to me, and I really appreciated that." That candidate, according to Frank Cardinale, won easily. He pounded the pavement and dirt paths; Republican, Democrats, significant others. If you have the time, then make the effort and keep on knockin'.

What party is that candidate in? Look around and try to find the name of the political party on lawn signs and billboards. It's rare that you would. Local candidates want their names known. Mentioning one's party limits one's appeal. **Be a universal door-knocker.** I've heard of candidates losing elections by one vote. They probably forgot to knock on that house two hundred yards in the woods.

Diana Spada suggests that candidates not knock on doors when wearing double-breasted suit jackets and extremely expensive, showy watches, as happened with one candidate. When she saw him, she said, "We need to talk. You need to take your jacket off and give me your watch. You're not wearing it till after you get elected (she knew the odds of his doing so)."

He said, "You don't understand. This was a birthday present from my wife."

She said, "**YOU** don't understand that most people in their lifetimes whom you're going to visit never saw a real one. So that's an example of what I call a 'Come to Jesus Moment.' Those are the kinds of niches I have and I'm not shy in saying it. It takes a certain kind of candidate to work with me.
And by the way, speaking of luxurious appearances: **Park the BMW, Mercedes, Jaguar, etc., and arrive in a modest vehicle.** I'm sure you understand the implications of that.

Reflection on a hood

Judge Anthony McGinty says, "You have to be able to see people, meet them and make a good impression, all in a few minutes." I asked if he had prepared and practiced from a script he prepared and he answered, "Yes, absolutely. It's very helpful to do so."

You have to know the issues of your campaign, so that when you are asked why you want to be running for your particular office, you will have a ready answer. You cannot stand there and fumble or hesitate and speak nonsensically with "ums, ughs, hmmmmms."

Memorize the few and most important issues in order to talk to people authoritatively… **NOT** condescendingly. People will sense your comfort, unease, arrogance, humility, warmth or deception immediately. Talk as if you were talking to a good friend. Make it short and sweet. There are lots of doors upon which to knock in the neighborhood. As Judge McGinty stated, **rehearse**. Do it in front of relatives or campaign people or in a mirror.

Your body language is as important as your little speech. When practicing, be aware of your flying hands, blinking eyes, foot movement and insincere laughter. Practice will help cure all that.

Judge McGinty says, "When knocking on doors, I start with an apology. It's an intrusion, They don't want people. Some have signs up that say, 'No Soliciting.' You want to be wearing casual clothes; a sweater, a jacket, a candidate's button." Ties are not necessary and might be perceived as off-putting. Jeans are okay, khakis are better, but open shirts should look neatly pressed. Dresses too short or tight are not acceptable. Looking too sexy is not of benefit. We know you look terrific, but downplaying your looks is much more professional and effective.

Judge McGinty: "I have in my hand some literature and I'd like to take a few minutes of your time and introduce myself and ask for your vote, and we'll talk so you can see what's going on. I'm not going to impose on you."

Ms. McGinty always backs a few steps away from the door after knocking. "I don't want to be in their face when they open the door. I campaigned with my baby on one of my campaigns. I parked the carriage at the end of the walk and then knocked on doors. If freaked people out that I was doing this— in a positive way!"

Ms. McGinty also stated, "**If you're afraid of the people and you are asking for their vote, you've got a serious problem.** A lack of trust means that you won't be able to make that vital, personal connection. I want you to vote for me as a person. I'm asking you to vote for me so I want you to know and see who I am.

"**It's important to make the effort**, one to one, to ask people for their vote. A vote is a precious thing and the voters you reach out to deserve to know the kind of person you are."

Judge McGinty relates it to body language. "For some people who don't like to touch, it's eye contact, handing kids balloons, distributing brochures, taking time to talk. Whatever makes that personal connection. For some people it's just the physical contact of a handshake, or as Ms. McGinty says, "Pressing the flesh. It's whatever makes that personal contact that registers in one's mind: It says that this is someone who is interested in me and interested in my vote. Whatever you do to make that connection is powerful. But it's respecting them and respecting the fact that they may be doing something else they want to do (at the time I'm knocking on their door), like watching the Super Bowl, and you're ringing the doorbell, trying to make the connection really quickly and then letting them get back to the game (or whatever else they seem to be doing)."

Determine a starting point and end point of the streets and targeted homes to be visited. Make a map or use a map. Map programs on cellphones are excellent. Sometimes the candidate will join you, and at other times, I suggest you always go with another person. If you are a female, have a male colleague accompany you or another female. If you are a male, do not go with a second male, as it's possibly too threatening to homeowners, especially in poorer neighborhoods. People run scared when they see strangers, who might be seen as detectives or government people at the door.

Put a smile on!!! Politeness is essential. If rejected, say "Thank you" without sarcasm and go on to the next home, but leave your material behind for them to possibly consider.

Hand out brochures, palm cards and little gifts, such as nail files, magnets, mirrors, brooms (yes, brooms) and pens, as examples. Kathleen (Kathy) LaBuda, county legislator in Sullivan County, NY, and her volunteers handed out pens when going door-to-door. She also handed out palm cards, but thinks that "people just throw the palm cards into the garbage, but they never throw out the pens and use them every day, so that our candidate's name is in front of them constantly as a reminder." She said that one should hand out really good quality, wider pens so that a candidate's name can be printed larger. Other items handed out by her and her volunteers were hats, mugs, tee shirts, if you can afford them, etc. "The bigger the race, the bigger the item. People like candy. Everybody likes candy, chocolate candy or mints with "Vote for _____ (your name)" printed on the packages. Give them something to eat or something to write with; pads to go along with the pens with your name on them, something they can use over and over."

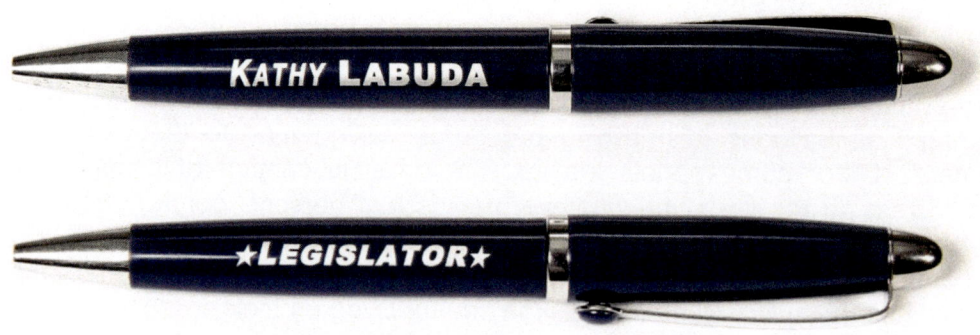

One candidate I photographed handed out small brooms he had imprinted with his name and slogan, "Sweep The Town Clean," (he won by a landslide). also mugs, tee shirts, if you can afford them, etc.

A palm card is generally postcard size (3.75"x6") or a bit longer (3.75"x7"). It should fit into a #10 envelope if ever being mailed in one. 4" extends a bit over the flap and is sloppy looking when sealed and that's why I recommend 3.75", instead of 4". They can also be 6"x9" or even larger, as illustrated here below.

Kathy LaBuda's palm card was an oversized 6"x11". Note that she was supported by three parties. She stated, "You cannot win a county-wide election if you don't have the extra party lines."

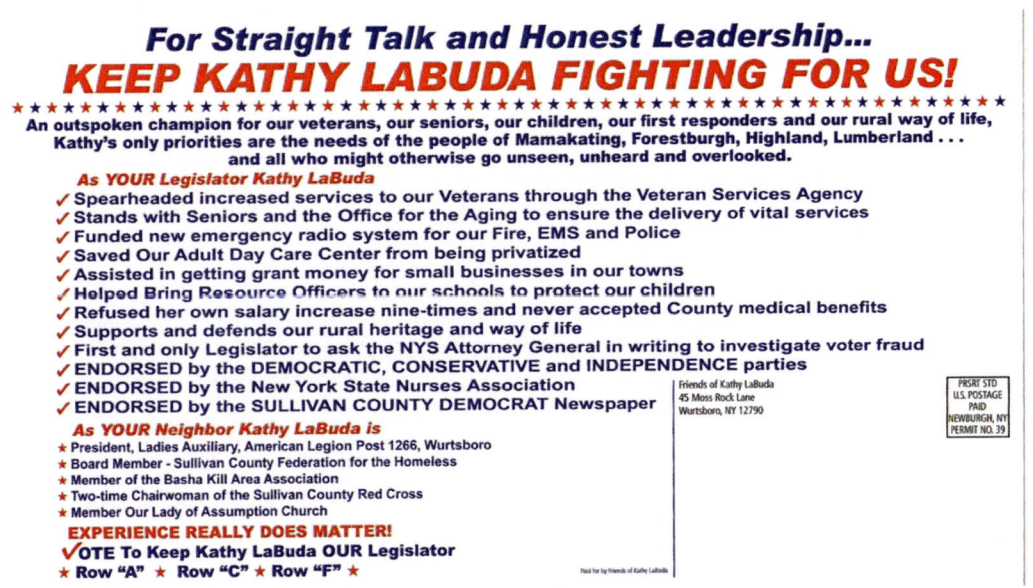

Palm card mailer, front and back

If the card is a mailer, room should be left on the bottom right for names and addresses and postal permit box for mass mailings. Do check with the Postal Service for the size requirements for appropriate postage, position and postal permit regulations. They have to be very specific. You would fill out a postal permit application with the Postal Service.

When Ulster County District Attorney candidate **Holley Carnright** first ran for office, he had bingo markers made with his name printed on them and went from bingo parlor to bingo parlor handing them out. His slogans on them were "Be a Winner" and "Vote for Safe Streets."

He always first asked permission to do that, and because the charities sold markers to patrons, Mr. Carnright made contributions to the various sponsoring charities so that they would not suffer a loss of income when he was permitted to distribute his markers.

He was thus able to target hundreds of people in a closed environment all at once, and that giveaway campaign proved to be highly effective. He won.

Bingo Marker

If a resident is not home, always leave a handwritten, **signed note** saying, **"Sorry I missed you."** It is important that it be handwritten and **NOT printed. Gloria Kantrowitz** says that the best time to go door to door was in the mornings and around dinnertime. "If people weren't home, I hung palm cards on doors with rubber bands. I had a 103 degree fever and still went door to door."

Ms. LaBuda declares that the most important aspect of connecting with voters is the old fashioned way, going door-to-door.

It's extremely important that candidates knock on every appropriate door.

Some candidates will never go door to door, but connect with constituents in other ways. They might personally invite constituents to special events or a caucus. They would write personal notes, which are always well-received and most impressive. When writing notes or walking through villages or small cities, greeting people, it's important to acknowledge people.

CHAPTER 25
THE WHOLE MESSAGE AND NOTHING BUT THE WHOLE MESSAGE, AND "DEAR NAME" LETTERS

Repetition breeds familiarity. One of my marketing research colleagues and advisor, the late Dr. Edwin Field of Field Associates, Monticello, NY, and advisor for numerous advertising campaigns, taught me years ago that the most effective ad campaigns were those that were repeated at least seven times. It was the best marketing lesson one could ever learn.

Control and develop the message: This is a coordinated effort of logo design, letter writing, phone messages, palm cards, brochures, business cards, ads, billboards, printed matter, website, blogs, Facebook, Twitter, LinkedIn, emails, etc.

Regarding billboards: If you are planning on having billboards, keep the message as large, simple and bold as possible. LESS IS MORE. One of the executives of a sign company, who was also on the national billboard association board, told me that the average time a driver had to look at and concentrate on a billboard, was between one and two seconds. Absolute simplicity is a necessity: photo, name, office and perhaps, a short slogan. Website, too, but less important. No one has time. Of course, if drivers are on that road repeatedly, they'll start to register the website in their minds.

But one candidate lamented to a supporter, a radio executive, that his opponent was killing him with billboard exposure, but the radio exec told him that after one or two viewings, nobody paid attention to the billboard and it just sort of faded into the landscape. Perhaps electronic billboards are much more visible and long-lasting in the publics' mind. They are certainly seen from greater distances. One should be aware that electronic billboard messages should display only one page. Multiple pages can be extremely distracting and dangerous for drivers, diverting their attention from the road.

Think of issues that would be of importance to constituents on palm cards: Always a headshot of the candidate on the front, a campaign slogan, important issues, photo on the back either alone and/or with his or her family, as large as possible, as well as perhaps, local phone numbers of police and fire departments (and 911), a yearly calendar, important holidays, **election day**, social services, senior citizens department, governmental departments' phone numbers and emails of local public servants, candidate's phone number and email for immediate access.

I'd say, with a wink and a smile, "Now don't go throwing that handsome/beautiful face out until you've given it a fair look. I'm a great guy/gal and I'm here because I can help you, and the truth is, I really need **your** help. This isn't a party issue. Besides, those emergency numbers and dates on my palm card will be very helpful for you." It might just turn a person.

Generally, one would list two or three important, local issues on palm cards and fliers. Chris Petsas, Chairman of Poughkeepsie's Common Council, listed eight issues. His opponent listed two or three.

His website expanded on those issues by stating that, "if you wanted to learn more about these and other issues as well, go to my website and see all the bullets on those. The palm card connected them to the website so they could get more information." **THAT** is why websites are so important for imparting information to constituents.

Richard Mathews's slogan on his palm cards and brochures was "Mathews Means Business." He used it in all his campaigns and it was highly effective. Come up with something catchy to help people identify and remember you. Some random others: "Make America Great Again," "A future to Believe In," "Reform, Prosperity and Peace," "Hope," "Time For a Change," "Working For You," "Working For a Better Future, Better County," "Independent Leadership." "A voice For You." There are tons on the internet if you cannot think of your own. And that's okay, BTW.

Judge Kane's giveaways were palm cards, tri-fold fliers and emery boards with his name on them. "Emery boards were great because decades later women were still walking around with their emery boards in their pocketbooks with my name printed on them."

Anthony T. Kane's first trifold flier distributed during his first judicial campaign. He served as a judge in various courts for 25 years, ending his career as a New York State Supreme Court Judge.

Fliers should include numerous photos of the candidate, especially a most prominent headshot, photos of family and prominent supporters, their short testimonials, as well location shots with candidate at sites of important issues, such as polluted streams, shuttered industrial buildings, etc. and even a **special recipe** with a photo.

You can send people my special home-baked, winning campaign bread recipe with **your** name on it if you'd like, which is the best bread ever. Email me and I'll be happy to share and send it to you. Set out that home baked bread at a coffee klatch or tea reception and you will never be forgotten. Email me at **mgphotoman@gmail.com** and write "Chef Mikey's **WINNING Campaign, Home-Baked Bread Recipe**" in the subject bar. I'll send it to you. It's another way to keep your name in front of voters. This idea has been used previously and effectively.

WINNING Campaign Bread by Chef Mikey

The idea is for people to retain your literature and not dump it in their garbage. Leave a blank space on the mailer for it to be used as a direct mail piece without the necessity of having to place it in an envelope. **Check with the post office to make sure your piece is designed properly for mailing and postage.**

Wealthier candidates will customize different mailers with specific issues featured prominently. Most often though, candidates will get by with just one mailer. It should not be too visually busy.
Elegant design, beautiful fonts, great writing and color photos will always stand out and create a most favorable impression. Mailers are ads for candidates.

Sample of the front of a campaign mailer. Candidate's info. on the back

Jeff Siegel, former candidate for the Sullivan County Legislature, felt that, "Coming up with the best looking logo for my campaign was most important. I was the most recognizable candidate and they knew what I was running for… County Legislature. With graphics and artwork that came up to brand me as running for office.

"And… in doing all of that was the photographer I chose to do take the proper professional headshots, which were used in conjunction with my logo." (Yours truly, M.G., of course).

Relationship with printers. Candidates should try to establish relationships with local printers. For one thing, it's "Shop Local" and you would try to give them the business, as opposed to sending your work out to online companies or out of area companies. You need a go-to printing executive to work with you. "Shopping Local" is critically important for those seeking political office. People need to know that you're supporting the local economy.

Since campaigns depend upon extremely tight deadlines for printed matter, there are times when your work must be done ASAP. Out of area printers simply cannot provide that service. You have to be able to have your campaign marketing people, or yourself, walk into a local print shop and almost walk out with your needed fliers, palm cards, postcards, bumper stickers, etc. It means establishing personal relationships and building mutual trust.

They'll do the work, you pay promptly. Ascertain though, that your print shop has high-speed, modern digital capabilities. Their being in the same party, or neutral, would be important to me as well. You don't want to think about someone "sabotaging" a job. It may be nothing, but these possible scenarios occur to me. I'm so paranoid.

"Dear Neighbor," letters

Dear _____< Name, (or neighbor, friend)

Hope all's well with you and your family.

Just wanted to let you to know that my good friend_____, has decided to run for councilman (or any other position) and I am volunteering for his/her campaign. He/she is incredibly experienced, having served (qualifications)_____.

I think he's/she's a terrific, caring guy/gal who is determined to better the community for all of us and I'm going to put some time in on his/her behalf.

If you also have any time to help, let me know, and if not, I hope you'll help spread the word supporting him/her. I wouldn't waste my time if I didn't think _____(Candidate's name) will make a great councilman (or deserve to be reelected.)

Warmest regards,
Your Name and position– Signed and typed

The personal letter to fellow constituents: Handwritten personal notes on behalf of the candidate are invaluable. These are the notes that will be most considered and discussed. It's friend to friends, relative to relatives and business friend to colleagues, and are most effective. Have your campaign manager work out a personal script and make sure words are spelled **correeectctily**.

You don't want the candidate to look bad and you don't need silent questions about the candidate's education and communication skills. Everyone has personal Christmas and other holiday lists, as well as many other addresses of local acquaintants in their computers or cellphones. It's a great way to start with those.

– Sample notes to strangers should state the candidate's strengths and experiences:
– Background, both educationally and professionally
– Years of experience
– Membership in various service, volunteer and charitable organizations and extent of involvement

Name the party if it's a majority party in the candidates' district. **Otherwise, don't mention it**. It could hurt the candidate and it's not necessary to do so. As I've mentioned, local, grassroots campaigns will often omit a candidate's party affiliation in order to appeal to a larger voter base. Party affiliations are less important than recognition by local citizens.

Phone campaigns: Phone calls should be short, no more than 30 seconds, and oh, so sweet. A little "sugar" goes a long way. Your voice has to smile and convey "sugar" on behalf of your candidate.

Along with the campaign manager and perhaps the candidate him or herself, phone volunteers should gather and rehearse their phone message. It is critically important that it be done well and confidently.

Take a copy of the phone message home afterward and practice, practice, practice it on your spouse, kids, lover or pet. We want your candidate to get to, if not Carnegie Hall, then at least city hall. Do it over and over again until it is perfected and have driven them totally crazy. Your voice has to smile, be charming and informative.

People must end up having the best feeling for your support of the candidate. Indifference and not practicing on the phone is a killer. It will simply turn people off. There goes a vote out the window and no desire to get to the voting booth for you as a consequence.

And please don't mumble or speak too quickly, and don't speak with a bagel in your mouth!

CHAPTER 26
THE OMG BEAUTIFUL SMILE FOR THE CAMERA

HEADSHOTS: LOVE AT FIRST SIGHT **They are the most critical first impressions that voters will see and to which they will be attracted.** Your headshots and campaign photos are absolutely crucial to the success of your candidacy. You must use a really good, talented, creative, professional photographer and not your husband, wife, boyfriend, girlfriend, child, uncle or friend to take your campaign photos using your cellphone or a little point and shoot camera. And please, forget the "selfie" shot. It's using a smartphone in a really dumb way. An excellent headshot is an investment in your political future.

"**Friendships you make are very important in politics**. Make sure the candidate is photographed with an incumbent in higher office. They all know what the game is that those pictures must be taken. Present yourselves professionally. Don't pick your teeth."
–Marcy Goulart, former president, Democratic Women, Ulster County, NY

Schedule your photo appointment(s) at your most energetic time of day or night. Actually, when your biorhythm tells you that you are feeling sensational, beautiful, handsome, sexy and ready to conquer the world. All that energy translates into much stronger headshots and gives you a tremendous psychological edge when beginning the photo session. **You need to create photographic pheromones** with these portraits so that voters will look at your photos and say, **"Yes, Yes, YES, I MUST** make sure you win. I cannot live another moment without you representing me" and then cast their vote for you. So dramatic, I am…

Studio backdrops are critical: Browns and tans, whether painted on canvas, or brown or tan seamless paper are not recommended. It makes a person's face blend and fade into the background, and that beautiful face of yours is lost to an adoring public, so eager to see you clearly.

Recommended are backdrops in the blues, both royal and navy and various shades of gray and black and white. These are **POWER COLORS**, and all of them cause you to become three-dimensional and **you will pop out of the background**. A photographer should know in advance the color of your hair so that he or she can have the right shade and colored backdrop ready.

If you are blonde, blond or gray, you need a darker backdrop. If your hair is dark, a lighter backdrop would be more appropriate. These combinations of hair color and background color dramatize your headshots immeasurably. A black background is very theatrical. You need to be seen instantly. People shouldn't have to squint to try to find you. It must be an "AH HA!!" immediate impression.

Studio lighting: Think of lighting as sculpture, molding your face. Using four lights in various ratios is ideal: A main light on the left with the most power, a second light on the right with half or quarter power, a light above one's head to illuminate hair (not too powerful), and a background light of half or quarter power to give a little zing to the background.

A couple of things to consider: If you're bald or seriously receding, don't let the photographer use a hair light. It just makes your head shine as brightly as an LED bulb and is murder to retouch perfectly. You know what they always say about light reflecting off bald heads. "It's blinding!" Who needs it? It's distracting and embarrassing. Bald headed people (I'm really getting there myself) are just as sexy, but need different, simpler lighting. Bald is beautiful, too (I keep telling myself).

Also, if one has a great hairdo, mostly ladies, but with men, too, of course, one should break the "rules" and shine that back background light right into the back of the person's head and create a kind of hair halo. It's very sexy and makes that person pop even more three dimensionally. It's movie star lighting, and you are reaching for the stars as well.

For added drama, one would have one of the front lights shut off and light a face with the one light from the side, about 45 degrees. This is easier to do with men, where shadows and some wrinkles enhance, rather than distract.

On women, try to soften the lighting with less shadows to de-emphasize facial imperfections. Sometimes, a lighting ratio of full power and the other on three quarter power softens a face but still allows for three dimensionality. Creative photographers (like me) will play with these lighting ratios. Most often, one will lower one's lights a bit to soften those shadows if there are serious wrinkles or bags under one's eyes.

If people wear glasses, make sure that your photographer is alert for glare in the lenses. If one is nearsighted, lights must be raised to avoid glare. It's a real pain. Be aware of excessive shadows on one's cheekbones. If one is farsighted though, it is much, much less of a problem to light them.

CHAPTER 27
POWER POSES & MICHELANGELO'S STATUE OF DAVID
(At Least, The Face)

An example of the ultimate, contrapposto power pose

Think of Michelangelo and his statue of David. If you haven't seen it, give it the old Google-oscopy. Fine arts majors at Boston University were taught about the ultimate Power Pose, known to us as *"contrapposto."*

It's when the head is turned one way and the shoulders somewhat in the opposite direction. It creates a physical tension and sense of anticipation. It makes you look much more formidable and powerful. And we used to think it was a kind of pasta in art school! Now I know, it's delicious in another way! And BTW, you can keep your clothes on, unlike "David," unless you're running for office in a nudist colony.

Power Poses: This isn't a high school portrait. A photographer should take many shots, not four or five or six and then, *"Next student, please."* This is really very serious stuff to think about. School photos often have the student facing straight ahead, shoulders aligned. It's boring, even with a cute smile.

Examples of professional power pose headshots

Turn one shoulder in one direction and your head in another. Tell the photographer what your best side is, if you have a side you prefer.
If your hair is parted on one side, try to be photographed from the side on which you have more hair.

To smile or not to smile? That is the question: Yogi would answer "YES." Give yourself lots of choices, and don't be scared to do both. Give all kinds of looks, the kinds that you give yourself when looking in the mirror. Be loose, be funny, be serious, be inquisitive, be alluring. Be professional. Flirt with the camera. Really, I'm serious. Do so. It's fun to do and will bring out the multiple aspects of your personality, as a result. The photographer is sure to get a bunch of very compelling shots, but be open with your poses.

Oh, and there's that magical scalpel called Photoshop to perform digital plastic surgery on you when all is said and done. It's very biblical when in the right surgeon's hands: It giveth and taketh and maketh you very, very happy with the final results, as displayed on your posters and printed material.

A refrain from a song I wrote just for you, sung to the tune of "Bye Bye Blackbird:"

"Retouch all those zits and moles
From your cheeks to your nose,
Byeeeee, byeeeee blackheads"

Remind your photographer that how you pose and how you are retouched in the studio should remain absolutely **PRIVATE**. Make that understood! Gossip is not allowed, nor the sharing of your photos on the internet without your permission.

CHAPTER 28
POWER CLOTHES AND CAMPAIGN APPEARANCE FOR PHOTOGRAPHY SITUATIONS

Clothes: What is the style of clothing you should be wearing?
Jacket worn by Richard Gillette, a member of The Sons of The Revolution of New York State

Wear the right clothes for each occasion. The four preferable, power colors are black, blue and gray, especially in Washington. Red is considered to be the fourth power color. I also very much like red outfits on women. In photos, light or white colored jackets also look good and professional.

For formal power headshots, when I take photographs, I prefer that men wear white or light blue shirts, dark jackets and conservative ties. Depending on what part of the country you're from, you might wish to wear a string tie and western shirt. If not sure about the tie, bring more than one to the studio and let your photographer help you select. Take photos with more than one tie. Take photos, too, if you prefer, that are also more casual without a tie. Your persona may be more of a country look with a much more casual shirt as well.

You might also want to take photos with cowboy hats. It all depends on a local style of acceptance. You might wear a Hawaiian shirt in Hawaii or in the South, but not in Texas I'd imagine, and visa versa.

Don't underdress, though. You're not communicating or respecting your constituents, and it creates the impression that you're talking down to them. You want to elevate yourself, look the role for which you're campaigning without turning people off. "My God, look what the hell he looks like!" You need to hear that like a hole in the head. Be sensible and dress smart for your position and locale.

For women, also dress appropriately for the position for which you're running. I've been told by the head of one of the local county parties, a woman, that female candidates should dress conservatively with understated hair and jewelry. If too much is worn, it might cause an undercurrent of resentment or derision among those who might not possibly afford such lavishness.

Strategist Diana Spada said, "We had a candidate for Family Court judge. She's very young and very, very, very pretty. And my 'Come to Jesus moment' with her was, 'People don't want to look at a Barbie doll. You're not a model. All I'm hearing is that you're gorgeous, you're gorgeous, you're pretty. Okay, you have to cut your hair.
– 'I don't want to cut my hair.' – 'We have to cut your hair. You have to get your hair cut.' So she cut her hair.

"You know, I don't want to look at you and see sex. I want to look at you and see a lawyer. I want to see glasses on. I want to see a suit. I want to see a more conservative person. That's what we're saying. You want to be a judge. You're 34 years old. That's a big step to make at 34 years old. Why should people trust you, and they're trusting you with their children. They don't want a Barbie doll. Most mothers with four kids at 34 don't look like you do. You don't want to lose the women's vote because you're too pretty." The candidate won handily.

Men should not wear big pinkie rings. They look too elitist and showy.

Makeup, of course, is essential, especially lipstick and/or gloss. In the studio, a no lipstick look makes for a much more bland photo and makes women appear drained. Even if it's applied sparingly, a bit of lip color makes one look more appealing and energetic.

Scarves are lovely and eye catching, but not those with overly bold patterns. Women can wear more colorful tops, but again, always bring at least one power outfit: dark, understated, elegant, yet very feminine. I do love red as well. We want women to look and feel their most beautiful and professional at the same time. Flaunt it within reason. Cleavage exposure is at your discretion. What else can I say about that?

Some women candidates or incumbents are known for the unique hairdos or hats they wear. By all means, remain in character or create a persona you've had in mind. Be courageous.

Be flamboyant, if that's the real you. It all stays in the studio, ethically, so play with it and be fearless. You're not obligated to select any of those, but at least you've experimented.

But if your campaign manager and intimate advisors suggest you change your look and hair for the campaign, you'd be wise to take their advice. It's their experience that counts most. For men, that might mean shaving off that beard or moustache. That look of a three day growth is totally UNacceptable.

Outdoor on-location campaign portraits
A lesson from a significant, personal experience: I spent a day some time ago photographing on–assignment for a member of The United States House of Representatives. We went from location to location throughout his home district, driven by one of his assistants, and before he reached each location, he changed his clothes in the car.

When we visited a particular farmer, he was wearing jeans and a chambray work shirt and work shoes for walking out in the black dirt onion fields, scooping up that rich dirt, smelling it while discussing farm issues with the farmer, who was dressed similarly. At a senior citizens complex, he changed into khakis and an open white short-sleeved shirt. He spoke at length with a number of people, sitting next to them or crouching down, engaged in conversation, hugging, kissing, hand holding, smiling, laughing.

At an elementary school, he changed shirts yet again and played with the kids and spoke to some teachers and administrators. Finally, at a large debate with a couple of his opponents, he changed into a black pinstriped suit, white long-sleeved, button down shirt, conservative tie, diagonally striped, and shiny black dress shoes.

He knew his constituents, his various audiences, and was the right person to everyone, meaning most impressive in his appearance at every occasion. He was considered a man of courage and great integrity and never lost an election in his many years serving his district in Congress. His name was **Benjamin Gilman**.

Family campaign portraits: These are more casual and most important for candidates. People love to see political families. Happy children sitting on laps tug at the heartstrings. Smiles and a feeling of affection are critical. Pets are a plus: besides dogs, horses, sheep, cows, etc. are always a plus, even if not pets. Yes, people even have pet cows. They are actually extremely affectionate. If a candidate is in dairy farm country, what the hell, why not??? It would certainly make a unique palm card or one of the photos on a brochure. Make sure to carefully choose and coordinate the style of dress for the portraits. Randomness is **NOT** acceptable, as the oddly dressed person or two would diminish the image of the candidate and take direct attention away from him or her.

People running for judgeships or other higher positions may choose to have more conservative family portraits so as to keep his or her image on a more formal level and not demean the position.

Find a pretty location and shoot with the sunlight behind you so that the sun's harsh shadows don't overwhelm anyone's face. The photographer should use a fill flash on the camera to soften the shadows and balance tones in the subject's face with natural, stronger light.

Photos of people receiving awards: When you receive a framed award certificate under glass, angle it downward a bit so that the photographer's flash doesn't create a glare on the glass and cause the writing to disappear.

Exhibit a bit of patience both when accepting the award and in posing with the people representing the organization. When shaking hands while accepting the award, hold the handshake for an extra couple of seconds, as well as posing with the other people while holding the downturned certificate. **This enables the photographer to grab a few extra, perfect shots**, and then eliminating those photo of people with eyes closed. Do not stand behind the podium when accepting an award. Walk to the side so that the photographer has a clear view. Please smile. Don't say "Cheese," even silently. I hate that word. And don't say "Bananas."

Photos illustrating controversial issues: Candidates are often photographed in locations where there are important and/or controversial issues on which they're taking a stand. These are highly effective in their ads and promotional material. My advice is NOT to smile. It's serious stuff and you wouldn't want to create a flippant impression. Again, choose your outfits carefully and **downplay** the glamour. Show your concern.

If you are photographing other people for your campaign, I'd strongly suggest you have those people sign model releases, giving you permission to use their photos for your publicity purposes.

When you're out on the campaign trail, dress for the weather and do not overdress. **Marcy Goulart** says, for example, "that if you're in a 4th of July Parade, and you're in 90 degree weather, by all means, roll up your sleeves and don't look so stuffy. Do not wear a suit and tie. Casual events do not demand that formality, and you would look totally out of place."

If it's a casual event, wear a business casual outfit, like a golf shirt and khakis. Her feeling, though, that even at casual events, county execs and higher should put on ties and jackets. Formal for women, as well. I don't necessarily agree. It all depends on the event. You simply have to use your own judgment and not underdress. Even the country's presidents take their ties and jackets off at certain public events. It's really whatever seems appropriate at the time.

CHAPTER 29
THE POWER OF THE WEB & DO-IT-YOURSELF VIDEOS

Illustration of the iconic "Mona Gorilla" on Facebook by Rick Meyerowitz

Truth be told: **First, special thanks to Kevin Brown,** President of CK Studios in Montgomery, NY, who is an Internet media expert and who has provided the bulk of this information. Mr. Brown has worked on numerous political campaigns and is the most sophisticated source of information in helping candidates get elected. He is also the most gracious fellow in sharing his technical information with me.

His suggestions are invaluable for the potential success of one's campaign. There has not been any money, nor promises passed between us of payment, just his interest in helping make my election guide that much better. He has asked for nothing in return. We're friends and professional colleagues and I don't want this to sound like a commercial for Mr. Brown. He is my main guide, though, and I shall be referring to him in this chapter. The writing, of course, is mine, except where quoted.

Ahhhhh, the Internet. Use it well and it will be **THE** most powerful tool you'll have at your disposal to dispense and share information about you and your campaign. I don't care how small a campaign you're running, you must create a website and use the other heavyweights, **Facebook, Twitter, Snap, Pinterest, Linkedin** and **YouTube.** They are the giants of social media and without them, you're in the minor leagues. Email is of use, as well, but limited to your contacts and your contacts' contacts.

When ready to announce your candidacy, Richard Croce says that YouTube, Facebook and other social media sites are the first places many candidates now use before anyplace else. Judicial candidates most often have announced on courthouse steps.

Family Court Judge Anthony McGinty, Ulster County, NY, says "The most powerful thing is my website. It's here that I talk about my platform."

When returning emails to numerous people, always, always, **always blind copy everyone.** It's "**Bcc**" when sending emails to more than one person. Do not share email addresses with anyone. It really gets people crazy to see their email addresses exposed to the public. They feel violated.

Creating a website can seem overwhelming, but there are professionals who can do this for you, Mr. Brown among them. If you want to tackle it on your own, "**WordPress**" is the do-it-yourself program to use. It allows you to change, add or delete information immediately and easily.

"**Websites must be relevant to what people are searching for**, in this case information about you and your campaign. They must be able to find that information quickly and easily, and all of this has to be compatible with smartphones and notepads. 50% of web browsing," according to Mr. Brown, "is now done on smartphones."

How do you get to the top of the list on Google? That is the "Holy Grail" when trying to get **search engine optimization.** No promises, but this is what Kevin Brown suggests: "Websites have to contain pertinent phrases so that when people are searching for you, your website will pop up. Candidates need to provide as many buzzwords and key phrases that are most important to them. There is special software available to assist candidates in obtaining the most powerful buzzwords and key phrases in every category."

"Unlike the old days of Internet searches, single search words are fairly useless. '**Long Tail Keywords**' are what one needs to target in order to get on the first search page. As an example: 'Widgets' will return millions of hits. 'Blue Widgets' narrows the search somewhat. 'Blue Plastic Widgets' narrows it further and '3 Inch Blue Plastic Widgets' is the Long Tail Keyword that will most likely help to get you on the first page of Google, especially if you had on your page all the attributes and benefits of '3 Inch Blue Plastic Widgets.' One would apply this to optimizing your webpage for your candidacy."

This is easy. Don't get overwhelmed.

For candidates, **"Long Tail Key Words"** are the ones first picked up by Google: The first entry is the candidate's name, then one word issues (elect, vote, candidate, economy, taxes, infrastructure, etc.) then **'Long Tail' Phrases, which YOU ABSOLUTELY NEED**, such as, "John Doe's position on high taxes, etc. What does John Doe have to say about taxes in Westchester County?" When describing your position on taxes or any other subject, you have to incorporate certain buzzwords in that description, as well as words the server computers detect.

When explaining any issues in detail, you should be using certain keywords and phrases that are determined by your Internet media expert. Google wants you to use their words for their own purposes, like ad words, but they are also your most important words **AND SHOULD BE USED IN YOUR VERY FIRST PARAGRAPH**. Always mention your locality, county and state in that first paragraph.

I've discussed placing column articles that are ads, and letters to the editor in local weekly magazines, as opposed to daily papers, which are discarded immediately. Weekly papers are kept around for a week and get read throughout the week. Websites, though, are always there for immediate, instant information.

The second most important necessity for your website is your BLOG. The blog should be a constant flow of information from you to the public. That is where the public goes to acquire information about your upcoming events, what you are currently doing, where you've been, whom you've met, and explanations of important issues as well as asking the public to join you at them. Photos are included in this.

On the homepage of your official website, you will need a headshot, professionally photographed and **NOT** a "selfie," nor a photo taken by a friend or spouse with a little point and shoot camera. **The headshot is your public's very first impression of you. Please do it right.**

If you insist on doing it yourself, then follow my detailed instructions in Chapter 27. It will be better than doing it without any knowledge of what would make a visual difference. Do not be penny wise and photo phoolish.

Take many photos and videos of events you've attended and with the people you've met: officials, party heavyweights, fellow citizens in professions whose votes you would need; chambers of commerce, various venues with senior citizens, vets, workers, schoolchildren, scouts, other people you perceive to be important or locations in your target sights, and select approximately six to eight for your homepage as a continuous looped slideshow. Photos with candidates shaking hands with constituents in all these locations are extremely important.

Remember family photos and CHOOSE THEM CAREFULLY, and make sure they are of the proper exposure and sharp focus. These photos should be seen for no more than 2 seconds at a time. People have no patience to linger over them, and they will be repeated continuously. Viewers can easily absorb the visual information in two seconds. They'll get the message.

If you have more than one page on your site, be generous with the numbers of photographs you would insert on each page. People will see more in photos, and follow that up with what you've written. Photos tell the story. What is it they say about the worth of a picture? How many words???? How many extra votes???? That's why lots of pictures count.

Every website needs a homepage, an "About Us" page, a "Terms of Service" page and a "Privacy Policy" Page. One also needs a "Contact Us" page for email and phone numbers. My suggestion is to put all your pertinent information, email address, phones and address on top of the homepage, besides the '"Contact Us" page. I think it's important to eliminate as many clicks as possible for voters who want to gather information and respond. Make it easy for them.

Also suggested for candidates besides the photos and videos are a logo, your biography, platform and an inspirational/philosophical statement.

You could also have videos on your website, and this is the beautiful thing about videos and the tie-ins with YouTube and Facebook:

This is important information. Don't get nervous. It's easy, but just follow the order in which the information is to be posted.

YouTube is the largest video sharing site in the world. It is owned by Google, and that means it's tied in with Google searches and shares them with your website. Facebook is the other social media site where videos are critical. The same applies to Facebook.

When posting (uploading) a video on YouTube, there is a box for the title of the video and then THE MOST CRITICAL STEP IS A BOX OF THE DESCRIPTION YOU WILL WRITE OF THE VIDEO:

"THE FIRST THING YOU HAVE TO DO IS TYPE IN YOUR WEBSITE IN THIS MANNER- HTTP://the name of yourwebsite.com (or whatever the end is, like .net or something else). This is a **hotlink** directly to your website and it is the very first thing people will see and read as well. One click and a viewer is on your website automatically. As I mentioned, this applies to Facebook, as well.

The magic of Facebook, when posting photos from your campaign is that it features facial recognition capabilities. What, you ask, is so important about that? If you're in a group of people already recognized elsewhere by Facebook, they will be recognized on your post with YOU.
It's a major plus to be seen with other well-known people in the community and it's done automatically.

Larger campaigns employ web experts to continually update their candidates' websites and blogs. That person or team can tie together all that information to Facebook, Twitter and YouTube. There is software available to do this and send it out to all those three social media sites.
Congressman Chris Gibson employs a social media coordinator and team to synchronize his posting information on social media: i.e. press releases and responses to those who responded by email to the information on his various sites.

Congressman Gibson stated that "Beyond mail, you also have the opportunity to telecom town halls, to reach a broader audience, and then, you can reach out to everybody, even the non-voters. And once I was elected, I served everybody, because I believe once the elections are over, the rule is to represent everyone in one's constituency, not just those who voted for you.

"This is the service which is providing a voice for people, regardless of party, regardless of how they vote, and I hope they vote, but even if they don't vote, I'm their voice."

When running campaigns that encompass large districts or states or all of the USA, the opportunity of speaking to many people person-to-person becomes impossible. TV appearances, debates, televised speeches and the Internet provide candidates with the means of addressing large numbers of voters. The revolution of social media has allowed those messages to be received in a most intimate manner. People are able to "talk back" and instantly voice their opinions.

In the past, it was letters to the editors, and now it's a direct one-to-one with the candidates.

Facebook is the biggest "yenta" in the universe. A "yenta" is a Yiddish word for gossip now relentlessly carried on through Facebook. You hear it all and see it all. It's an open window and open door for people both sharing and exposing their most intimate thoughts with all their friends. It's really pretty mesmerizing (and so much fun with the stuff people want to share) once you get into it and that is why it is so critically important for candidates and incumbents to use it.

Richard Croce talks of the importance of social media. He states that, "A candidate cannot meet everyone, but you can meet many more through social media. Most people today don't go to barbecues. They get very few people and they're the people who will vote for you if they're members of your party. **Facebook is the only way to go.** Twitter needs followers. Supposedly, there is a way where you can buy email lists of 'most likely voters' that is pretty comprehensive. It's from a private company."

As a candidate, you have an open outlet to share your philosophy, platform, thoughts on issues, and political and family experiences. You can take surveys on issues that concern constituents, and those will aid you in forming the two or three most important campaign issues to be focused upon. One would want to keep the list as short as possible so as to not overwhelm voters. You will also be able to put out the call for volunteers throughout your voting area.

Former Town of New Paltz, NY Supervisor **Susan Zimet**, is extremely wary of the abuse and lies emanating from social media, and how it is affecting local political discourse as well as nationally. "People are using social media and they don't have to go to a board meeting to say things. They attack you on social media instead, and the more they lie, the more it sounds like the truth.

"What is happening now and so scary is that we have people who've grown up on social media and they'll come to a town board meeting and say, 'Well, on social media, they say 'blah blah blah blah blah.' You don't have to go to a board meeting, stand up, face the cameras and say something. Instead, they attack you on social media and if they attack you enough, it becomes the truth. It's a coward's way out.

"**We're not running the town on social media.** We're running the town at the board's table and we're not going to make decisions based on what people say on social media. What's happening now is that we have a bunch of kids who grew up in the world of social media and they're the ones who are actually stepping into political offices. We really have a great fear for the future, and quite frankly, it's because they're not interacting with each other.

It is one thing to say something mean and have to look into the eyes of the person you just hurt, versus hiding behind a computer screen. And the collateral damage is that it also inhibits people from running for office because they're going to be savaged on social media, and they want no part of it. The bullies win.

"**Social media is really bastardizing politics.** FDR was the radio president, John F. Kennedy was the TV president and Obama was the social media president. People are overwhelmed, people are hurting so much, but they don't have time to get involved. And now they're scared to get involved."

Sullivan County Legislator Kathy LaBuda agrees: "People now go on a site and make negative comments and you can't respond. I'd have a press conference and everyone said 'take the high road' and I do not listen. If someone said something negative, you immediately hold a press conference and take them on because in the old days, you would take the high road because you wanted to act like you were above that. Now, because of social media, nope, never take the high road, never."

MG: "If somebody's lying, how do you countermand that negative campaigning?"

Ms. LaBuda: "If people are lying about you on Facebook, for instance, first hold a press conference and tell people this is absolutely not true! Not only that, you send out a form letter: 'My opponent said ABC about me and it's absolutely false.'"

MG: "What do you think is the most effective way of counter attacking, a letter or press conference? Do you think Facebook is the most powerful tool on the Internet?"

Ms. LaBuda: "I want to say no. In my opinion, it's a different generation now. I'm not on Facebook, but I think the most effective response would be a press conference, and that's because you'd have the media there and the media's gonna do the news."

MG: "You'd get in touch with newspapers, TV, radio?"

Ms. LaBuda: "Absolutely! They're all gonna come. Most of the time, they're honest and they want to hear about your opponent. They want to know the truth. They want to do a story. That's why I will hold a press conference. Absolutely! Absolutely! Never wait.

Ms. LaBuda-: "After the press conference, we write a letter saying 'My opponent made false comments about me.' If the main newspaper, The Record, came to my press conference and published my story about my opponent saying ABC lies, that might be enough. They would call my opponent and ask 'Why did you say that?' Your opponent's not gonna lie. Being in the paper is your first line of defense."

MG: "What about your own email list against the lies?"

Ms. LaBuda: "If you have an email list, you go right on it immediately. Absolutely.

"Twitter and all that stuff the young kids do, absolutely. But I'm not on it and I don't think it's good. As a county legislator I have no blemishes on my record and set the record straight. That's not personal. This is about your job. That's my legacy. I'm clean."

MG: "But really, what you're saying about not taking the high road, is actually that you feel you must counteract the lies that are told about you, in a very aggressive manner. 'You mean, 'doing battle?'"

Ms. LaBuda: "Yes, absolutely."

However, social media CANNOT be ignored in one's campaign. Whatever the trepidation, communicating one's message through all the sites in social media is of critical importance. Whether one's campaign is for the country's presidency or for a local, grassroots position, the web is king and queen. It's the fastest way to communicate your position to the largest possible audience. It is a powerful communication tool when used effectively. **It will help you WIN!!!**

For judges, though, Facebook is extremely problematic. Judge McGinty explained that, "Facebook, though, is a particularly difficult problem for sitting judges, because as a judge you're not supposed to be communicating with people whose cases are in front of you, and when you open up a Facebook page when you campaign, you're really giving lots of people an opportunity of directly communicating with you. If you do have a Facebook page, it's a problem, and you have to have someone, **not you**, monitoring the page all the time to make sure that the people who are trying to communicate are not the people who should not be communicating with you.

"**You have to have a screening mechanism** so that communications that come to you through Facebook, don't come to you directly."

Ms. McGinty said, "As an example: If someone has a custody suit in front of you, you don't want them to communicate with you."

"You have to be careful if you have a Facebook page. If someone posts something negative on your Facebook site, you have to decide if you're going to leave it there, etc. You really cannot respond."
Twitter, also sensational for sending non-stop messages, is limited to 140 characters initially, but there is a "Read More" button that allows you to add more. Even on Facebook, there is the "Read More" button to expand your message.

What a candidate should do is encourage his or her online contacts to get in touch with their friends and associates to spread the word, encouraging them to link on to your site for a steady stream of campaign information. It's exponential and that is the beauty of Facebook and Twitter in generating interest in a candidate.

The key phrases on Facebook and Twitter are the must-have links, which are **"Join Us On Facebook" and "Follow Us On Twitter."** These are dynamic, instant means of communicating back and forth, but do not negate the absolute importance of your website in imparting information about you, your platform, altruistic statement, professional headshot, family photos, photos on location related to issues, the beauty of the area, etc.

What's a backlink, and why are backlinks so important for you to Google?
They're incredibly important to you. Who knew? Ya live, ya learn.

Backlinks are like votes, sort of like a private election campaign, but online. Google recognizes and indexes all your key phrases (Remember, I mentioned Buzzwords and Long Tail Phrases?), which can be in any order. **WHAT IS IMPORTANT IS THAT THOSE BACKLINKS BE MOST RELEVANT TO YOUR CAMPAIGN** in order to garner the most votes from Google.

Backlinks are endorsements from other pertinent sites that have agreed to include your website on their sites, such as a county tourism board, chamber of commerce, fire department, or other community organizations. It is a gift from them to include your site on theirs. They count as **"VOTES"** and the more you get, the greater the chances are of your **"winning,"** meaning the higher your placement on Google. **Those relevant endorsements will get double the votes from Google.**

If you receive backlinks from a diner you frequent, or hairdresser or dry cleaners, they would not be considered to be as relevant and would only earn one vote. It's important to concentrate on getting relevant websites to backlink with you. You might have fewer backlinks, but if they are the most relevant ones, you would be ranked higher on Google.

You have to ask them personally and provide them with pertinent information about you and your campaign and platform, as well as your own website for them to evaluate. They would do it by their own internal vote on a non-partisan basis. Do show your appreciation if approved. **It is a really big deal.**

Repeating myself regarding VIDEO: In our digital day and age, the Internet is critical in getting your message out and people want to see you in action, interacting with people. Remember to always do videos when on the campaign trail so that you can punch them easily onto Facebook, YouTube, etc. Cellphones can provide you with all the quality you'd ever need and they're so much fun to use. Make a small jpeg to automatically go on every email after your signature. Be sure to include all pertinent information with the photo after you've signed your emails: phones, address, website, email (again), slogan. You always want to include all that information to make it as easy as possible for people to reach you or a staff member.

Of course, if you can afford professionals to do all this, by all means, hire them! Just do as much as you can yourself, especially when you're out at events while campaigning.

CHAPTER 30
THE SHORTEST & MOST IMPORTANT CHAPTER YOU'LL EVER READ

Never forget the "MAGIC WORDS:"

Please
Thank you
No thank you
You're welcome

They work wonders!

CHAPTER 31
THE DAY OF RECKONING, ELECTION DAY

Election Day: The years, months, weeks of endless hot dogs, cups of crappy coffee, cold pizza, takeout Chinese, shad roe, half eaten sandwiches, billboards, palm cards, fliers, mailings, lawn signs, meetings, events, speeches, more speeches, interviews, letters to the editors, handshakes and kisses, upset stomachs, little sleep, insomnia, cold sweats, self-doubt, the shakes, sore feet, hoarse voices, swollen hands, sweaty clothes, endless miles, endless smiles, endless campaigning, endless, endless, endless, endless every mind boggling detail, endless. And it's not over till the polls close.

At the last moment, your volunteers and staff can mean the difference between winning and losing First of all, they cannot electioneer closer than the lawful required distance at the polling stations. At the polling stations, they hand out fliers and palm cards, "Vote for my candidate," displaying the party lines on which your candidate is listed on the ballot.

It is imperative that your volunteers, on shifts if necessary, **remain at the polling places from the time they open till the time they CLOSE. Make sure your representatives are dressed well. You don't want schlumpy-looking people handing out your literature, which makes people really wonder.**

One of my interviewees, but who did not want to be identified, although extremely knowledgeable, stated that, "Standing out there, handing out literature, could decide the election by people who never knew what your office was or who you were until you handed them something outside the polling place and you saying, 'Please vote for my candidate for whatever the office is.

That's one of the ways you **WIN THE ELECTION**, and they'll say, 'Okay, I'll vote for that person'. So that does count for something, and that's just the ground operations. That's having volunteers and staff at every single polling place in whatever the size of the district. And it does work!"

The importance of getting out the vote is this: If a registered voter decides he or she hates each candidate and decides not to vote, period, then that voter is really casting his or her vote for the "enemy."

One has to make a decision and not throw that most privileged act in a democracy out the window. One has to decide whom he or she hates less and vote for that candidate. Voting for an obscure candidate who has absolutely no chance whatsoever is not a protest vote. It's a ridiculous act of folly. If one decides not to vote at all, it's simply really voting for the candidate you hate more. It's something voters should be made aware of. Candidates should make voters aware of this.

Little innocuous things can make a difference in influencing a voter's decision, like your own appearance, or smile, or that of your volunteer's, when handing out the campaign literature. People want to do their civic duty, but they are sometimes on the fence and do not know whom to vote for. It's your responsibility to influence their decision, even at the last second before walking the gangplank to the voting booth. This technique might just mean the difference between your winning or losing, by getting voters to decide to cast those potentially winning votes **for you.**

CHAPTER 32
LEAVE NO VOTE UNTURNED

Racing to vote or running for re-election

When the polls close, do make sure that your staff and selected volunteers are present when the votes are counted.

This is especially true when absentee ballots are opened and counted. I say trust no one. Make sure your own people are present, as well as other party officials.

Remember that elections can be won or lost by the numbers of absentee ballots that were cast, and more often than not, by scant numbers. You must be proactive and verify the count.

Don't mean to sound crazy. I just like to know what's going on and that there's no hanky-panky with short counts.

You're the super salesman or saleswoman and you're appealing to last minute shoppers, voters running to vote for you, **THE** most attractive candidate in the field.

It doesn't matter if "Each candidate is lacking something the opposing candidate doesn't have," as **Stanley "Yogi" Rubin** of Ellenville, NY, so wisely stated. It only matters that people get off their rear ends and cast their votes. Those lazy voters have to be made aware of the critical role they play when voting, and if one's volunteers have to carry them on their backs to the polling station, then carry they must.

In the meantime, other volunteers and staff are manning the phones, frantically reminding the lazy or forgetful voters to get out and vote. Hopefully, you'll be able to provide transportation to those in need of a ride, especially if the weather is inclement. Voters, especially elderly voters, are reluctant to drive in bad weather, and if you have a bunch of volunteers with cars, driving them could mean the difference of that one winning or losing vote. **We want winners benefitting from this book.**
You're making last minute speeches, running from one place to another, and your family is doing everything it can in a myriad of ways to help, as well.

And then…10, 9, 8, 7, 6, 5, 4, 3, 2, 1. **That's it, folks!**

Polls closed!

Your supporters are at election headquarters or the reception in the hotel or restaurant or bar, waiting for the final word from the Board of Elections or TV or computer, and you probably have two versions of a speech in your pocket, unless, of course, you're confident enough to guess the (**WINNING**) outcome.

The "Super Bowl" game is over at last!
What a grind it has been! It's either tears or cheers.
Please don't bite those nails!
I hope you won!
If so, you EARNED THAT VOTE, big time!
Congratulations from me!!!
I absolutely love all that confetti and balloons
and great, happy, foot stompin',
hand clappin' music, too!!!
Hope I'm invited to your victory party!
I'd love to share it with you and give you a
Great, big (appropriate) HUG!!

Michael Gold,
Citizen

CHAPTER 33
A TOAST TO THE WINNERS
The legendary Steve Jobs summed it up perfectly:

"Here's to the crazy ones, the misfits, the rebels, the troublemakers, the round pegs in the square holes... the ones who see things differently.

They're not fond of rules. You can quote them, disagree with them, glorify or vilify them, but the only thing you can't do is ignore them because they change things...

They push the human race forward, and while some may see them as the crazy ones, we see genius, because the ones who are crazy enough to think that they can change the world, are the ones who do."

My immense gratitude to the following contributors who selflessly gave their time and expertise in helping this book become a reality:

Chris Gibson, congressman, House of Representatives, for the 19 District, NY
Michael P. Hein, county executive, Ulster County, NY
Frank Cardinale, chairman, Democratic Party, Ulster County, NY,
Adele B. Reiter, deputy county executive and Chief of Staff, Ulster County, NY
Elliott Auerbach, county comptroller, Ulster County, NY
Victor Work, commissioner, Board of Elections, Ulster County, NY
Anthony T. Kane, judge, NY State Supreme Court & previously, Family Court, Sullivan County, NY (retired)
Anthony McGinty, Family Court Judge, Ulster County, NY
Sara McGinty, judge, Surrogate's Court, Ulster county, NY, attorney and former town judge, Rosendale, NY
Marcy Goulart, former president, Democratic Women, Ulster County, NY
Richard Mathews, chairman, board of supervisors, Ulster County, NY & Commissioner of Jurors, Ulster County, NY (retired)
Richard Croce, campaign manager for numerous judicial & district attorney campaigns
Diana Spada, campaign advisor and "Flint" Spada, her sulphur crested cockatoo
Ashley Dittus, deputy commissioner, Board of Elections, Ulster County, NY
Jodi Longto, volunteer
Kevin Brown, web and media master, CK Studios, Montgomery, NY
Kathleen (Kathy) LaBuda, former county legislator, Sullivan County, NY, campaign strategist
Hillel Hoffman, retired attorney, New York City
Greg Helsmoortel, town supervisor, Saugerties, NY
Daniel Torres, town councilman, New Paltz, NY
Harvey Lippman, treasurer and campaign advisor for California Governor Jerry Brown and the late New York Congressman, Allard Lowenstein, New York
Chris Petsas, Chairman, Common Council, Poughkeepsie, NY
Isaac "Yits" Kantrowitz, village judge, Woodridge, NY, and town judge, Town of Fallsburg, NY (retired)
Gloria Kantrowitz, member, Village Board, Woodridge, NY and volunteer
Sally Cross, former campaign organizer
Linda Gold, great wife, copy editor
Hanna Kisiel, my professional editor, proofreader and wonderful friend
Frederic Mayo, clinical professor of Hospitality and Tourism Management, New York University and co-author with Michael Gold of *Modern American Manners: Dining Etiquette for Hosts and Guests*,
Mark Sherman, former town councilman, New Paltz, NY
Sherry Giamichelle, model for power pose headshot
Jeff Siegel, former candidate for county legislator, Sullivan County, NY
Burt Gold, terrific brother and marketing consultant
Mark Resnick, terrific friend and advisor
David Krikun, professor of American History, SUNY New Paltz. NY (retired) and political advisor
Phyllis Freeman, professor of Psychology, SUNY New Paltz, NY and advisor
Robert Osgood, legal consultant
Gabrielle Brown, personal editor and fabulous daughter
Dane Brown, personal reader and model for power pose headshot
Charles Heenan, legal advisor and copy reader
Phyllis Rubin, copy reader
Arianne Gold, copy reader and fabulous Daughter
Nancy Kane, interviewee and volunteer for Judge Anthony Kane
Joan McDonald, director of volunteers, New York City (retired)
James McDonald, interviewee and husband to Joan McDonald
Martin Walker, literary and market research/media consultant
Stanley "Yogi" Rubin, director, Jewish Cemetery, Ellenville, NY
Rick Meyerowitz, political illustrator of *Mona Gorilla*, author and consultant
Gerald Benjamin, associate vice president, Regional Engagement & Director of the Center for Research, Regional Education & Outreach, SUNY New Paltz, NY
Alan Kraus, contributor of chicken quote
Burt Gulnick, campaign treasurer
Richard Gillette, Hurley, NY, proudly wearing the American flag jacket
Kathleen Brandes, CPA PC, Monticello, NY
Juniper Brown, flag artist

Juniper Brown, four years old: "I love American flags, Grampie."

"Democracy is the government of the people,
by the people, for the people."
President Abraham Lincoln

EARN THAT VOTE is available personally through **amazon.com** or through me. If ordered through me, I will inscribe the book to you or to whomever you're going to give it as a gift.

©2017 Michael Gold
1 Jacobs Lane, New Paltz, NY 12561
845 255 5255
EarnThatVote.com
mgphotoman@gmail.com
All rights Reserved. Reproduction in print or electronically is strictly forbidden.

Made in the USA
Middletown, DE
06 January 2017